2 **Discovering FRENCH** *Today!*

Blanc

Lectures pour tous

with Test Preparation

HOLT McDOUGAL

 HOUGHTON MIFFLIN HARCOURT

Printed in the U.S.A.

ISBN 978-0-547-87238-4
8 9 10   0928   21 20 19 18 17
4500685617   A B C D E F G

Table of Contents

Lectures supplémentaires

Academic and Informational Reading 155

Introducing *Lectures pour tous*

Lectures pour tous
is a new kind of reading text.
As you will see, this book helps
you become an active reader.
It is a book to mark up, to
write in, and to make your
own. You can use it in class
and take it home.

Reading Skills Improvement—in French *and* English

You will read selections from your textbook, as well as
great literature. In addition, you will learn how to understand
the types of texts you read in classes, on tests, and in the
real world. You will also study and practice specific strategies
for taking standardized tests.

Help for Reading

Many readings in French are challenging the first time
you encounter them. ***Lectures pour tous*** helps you
understand these readings. Here's how.

Avant de lire The page before each reading gives you
background information about the reading and a key to
understanding the selection.

Reading Strategy Reading strategies help you decide
how to approach the material.

What You Need to Know A preview of every selection
tells you what to expect before you begin reading.

Reading Tips Useful, specific reading tips appear at
points where language is difficult.

À réfléchir... Point-of-use, critical-thinking questions help
you analyze content as you read.

À marquer This feature invites you to mark up the text by underlining and circling words and phrases right on the page.

> ***Grammaire*** As you read, this feature highlights key grammar concepts.

> ***Vocabulaire*** This feature helps you with the new vocabulary as you read the selection.

> ***Analyse littéraire*** This feature appears in the *Lectures supplémentaires* section and encourages you to focus on one aspect of literary analysis as you read.

Reader's Success Strategy These notes give useful and fun tips and strategies for comprehending the selection.

Challenge These activities keep you challenged, even after you have grasped the basic concepts of the reading.

Vocabulary Support

Mots clés Important new words appear in bold. Their definitions appear in a *Mots clés* section at the bottom of any page where they occur in the selection. You will practice these words after the selection.

Vocabulaire de la lecture Vocabulary activities follow each selection and give you the opportunity to practice the *Mots clés.* Active vocabulary words appear in blue.

Comprehension and Connections

Tu as compris? Questions after each selection check your understanding of what you have just read.

Connexion personnelle These short writing activities ask you to relate the selection to your life and experiences to make what you have read more meaningful.

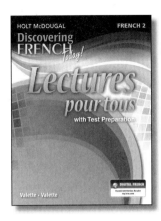

Links to *Discovering French, Today!*

When using ***Discovering French, Today!,*** you will find ***Lectures pour tous*** to be a perfect companion. ***Lectures pour tous*** lets you mark up the *Interlude* selections as you read, helping you understand and remember more.

Read on to learn more!

Academic and Informational Reading

Here is a special collection of real-world examples—in English—to help you read every kind of informational material, from textbooks to technical directions. Why are these sections in English? Because the strategies you learn will help you on tests, in other classes, and in the world outside of school. You will find strategies for the following:

Analyzing Text Features This section will help you read many different types of magazine articles and textbooks. You will learn how titles, subtitles, lists, graphics, many different kinds of visuals, and other special features work in magazines and textbooks. After studying this section you will be ready to read even the most complex material.

Understanding Visuals Tables, charts, graphs, maps, and diagrams all require special reading skills. As you learn the common elements of various visual texts, you will learn to read these materials with accuracy and skill.

Recognizing Text Structures Informational texts can be organized in many different ways. In this section you will study the following structures and learn about special key words that will help you identify the organizational patterns:
• Main Idea and Supporting Details
• Problem and Solution
• Sequence
• Cause and Effect
• Comparison and Contrast
• Persuasion

Reading in the Content Areas You will learn special strategies for reading social studies, science, and mathematics texts.

Reading Beyond the Classroom In this section you will encounter applications, schedules, technical directions, product information, Web pages, and other readings. Learning to analyze these texts will help you in your everyday life and on some standardized tests.

Test Preparation Strategies

In this section, you will find strategies and practice to help you succeed on many different kinds of standardized tests. After closely studying a variety of test formats through annotated examples, you will have an opportunity to practice each format on your own. Additional support will help you think through your answers. You will find strategies for the following:

Successful Test Taking This section provides many suggestions for preparing for and taking tests. The information ranges from analyzing test questions to tips for answering multiple-choice and open-ended test questions.

Reading Tests: Long Selections You will learn how to analyze the structure of a lengthy reading and prepare to answer the comprehension questions that follow it.

Reading Tests: Short Selections These selections may be a few paragraphs of text, a poem, a chart or graph, or some other item. You will practice the special range of comprehension skills required for these pieces.

Functional Reading Tests These real-world texts present special challenges. You will learn about the various test formats that use applications, product labels, technical directions, Web pages, and more.

Revising-and-Editing Tests These materials test your understanding of English grammar and usage. You may encounter capitalization and punctuation questions. Sometimes the focus is on usage questions such as verb tenses or pronoun agreement issues. You will become familiar with these formats through the guided practice in this section.

Writing Tests Writing prompts and sample student essays will help you understand how to analyze a prompt and what elements make a successful written response. Scoring rubrics and a prompt for practice will prepare you for the writing tests you will take.

Reading Strategy

This feature provides reading tips and strategies that help you effectively approach the material.

What You Need to Know

This section provides a key to help you unlock the selection so that you can understand and enjoy it.

Avant de lire   *Quatre surprises*

Reading Strategy

COMBINE STRATEGIES Put together the reading strategies you have practiced.

1. Look at the title and subtitles to predict the reading's theme.
2. Skim the reading to get a general idea of the content.
3. Use context clues to help you make intelligent guesses about new words.

Predict	Theme:
Skim	General Idea:
Use Context Clues	New Words:

What You Need To Know

Most inhabitants of Paris live in apartments. The typical apartment building has a **concierge** who lives on the ground floor, called the **rez-de-chaussée.** The **concierge** keeps the common areas clean and generally watches over the comings and goings of the residents. Most Paris apartment buildings also include an extra floor above the usual residences. This upper floor includes rooms that come with some of the more expensive apartments—rooms that are often converted to student rooms, or **chambres d'étudiants.** These rooms are also known as **chambres de bonnes,** or maids' rooms.

Unité 3
Quatre surprises   21

À réfléchir...

Point-of-use questions check your understanding and ask you to think critically about the passage.

1. What mistakes do Paul and David make? Check two. **(Summarize)**

☐ They didn't bring a hostess gift to Nathalie.

☐ They had written down the wrong street address.

☐ They arrived on the wrong day.

☐ They didn't introduce themselves to Nathalie's aunt.

☐ They entered the wrong apartment.

2. How would you characterize the type of reception the two Americans received in Paris? **(Infer)**

_____

_____

_____

▥ À MARQUER ▷ **GRAMMAIRE**

In this unit, you've learned about the various uses of the definite, indefinite, and partitive articles. Look at the boxed sections of the text and note the various examples of how all three are used. Underline an example of each and write them here:

Definite Article: _____

Indefinite Article: _____

Partitive Article: _____

22 **Lectures pour tous**

Quatre surprises

L'invitation

Paul et David sont deux étudiants américains. Avec l'argent qu'ils ont économisé cette année, ils ont décidé de passer un mois en France. Ils viennent d'arriver à Paris.
5 Malheureusement, ils n'ont pas d'amis français.

    PAUL: Tu connais des gens à Paris?

    DAVID: Non, je ne connais personne. Et toi?

10   PAUL: Moi non plus. Attends, si! Ma soeur Christine a une correspondante[1] française qui habite à Paris. Je crois[2] que j'ai son nom dans mon **carnet**
15   **d'adresses.**

Paul regarde dans son carnet d'adresses.

    PAUL: Voilà. La copine de ma soeur s'appelle Nathalie Descroix. J'ai son numéro de
20   téléphone…

    DAVID: Eh bien, téléphone-lui!

[1] pen pal   [2] believe, think

MOTS CLÉS
  un carnet d'adresses address book

Discovering French, Nouveau! Level 2

▥ À MARQUER ▷ **GRAMMAIRE**

This feature asks you to notice how a particular grammar concept from the *leçon* is illustrated. Underlining or circling the example makes it easy for you to find and remember.

READER'S SUCCESS STRATEGY

Notes like this one provide ideas to help you read the selection successfully. For example, some notes suggest that you fill in a chart while you read. Others suggest that you mark key words or ideas in the text.

MOTS CLÉS

Important vocabulary words appear in bold within the reading. Definitions are given at the bottom of the page.

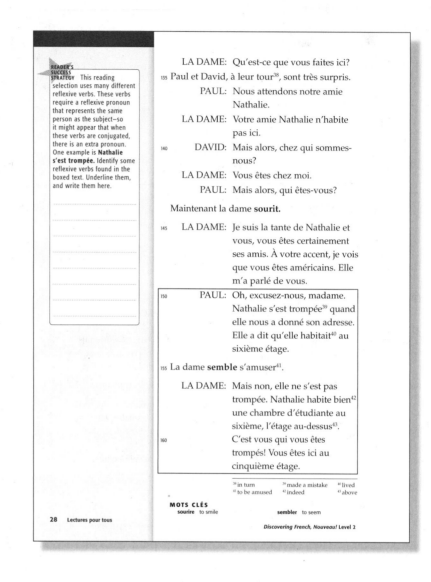

READER'S SUCCESS STRATEGY This reading selection uses many different reflexive verbs. These verbs require a reflexive pronoun that represents the same person as the subject—so it might appear that when these verbs are conjugated, there is an extra pronoun. One example is **Nathalie s'est trompée.** Identify some reflexive verbs found in the boxed text. Underline them, and write them here.

_____

_____

_____

_____

LA DAME: Qu'est-ce que vous faites ici?

135 Paul et David, à leur tour[38], sont très surpris.

PAUL: Nous attendons notre amie Nathalie.

LA DAME: Votre amie Nathalie n'habite pas ici.

140 DAVID: Mais alors, chez qui sommes-nous?

LA DAME: Vous êtes chez moi.

PAUL: Mais alors, qui êtes-vous?

Maintenant la dame **sourit.**

145 LA DAME: Je suis la tante de Nathalie et vous, vous êtes certainement ses amis. À votre accent, je vois que vous êtes américains. Elle m'a parlé de vous.

150 PAUL: Oh, excusez-nous, madame. Nathalie s'est trompée[39] quand elle nous a donné son adresse. Elle a dit qu'elle habitait[40] au sixième étage.

155 La dame **semble** s'amuser[41].

LA DAME: Mais non, elle ne s'est pas trompée. Nathalie habite bien[42] une chambre d'étudiante au sixième, l'étage au-dessus[43]. 160 C'est vous qui vous êtes trompés! Vous êtes ici au cinquième étage.

| [36] in turn | [39] made a mistake | [40] lived |
| [41] to be amused | [42] indeed | [43] above |

MOTS CLÉS
sourire to smile   **sembler** to seem

28   Lectures pour tous

Discovering French, Nouveau! Level 2

DAVID: Au cinquième étage? Je ne comprends pas! Nous avons compté les étages.

165

LA DAME: Votre erreur est bien excusable. Notre premier étage en France correspond au deuxième étage américain. Ainsi, vous avez pensé être au sixième étage. En réalité, vous êtes seulement au cinquième.

170

PAUL: Ça, par exemple[44]!

DAVID: Et le repas?

175

LA DAME: Je l'ai préparé pour des amis qui viennent passer la journée à Paris.

PAUL: Et la note sous le tapis?

LA DAME: Je l'ai écrite pour dire à mes amis que… Mais, au fait[45], où sont-ils?

180

Le téléphone sonne à nouveau[46]. La dame va répondre. Elle revient au bout[47] de quelques minutes.

185

LA DAME: Ce sont justement mes amis qui viennent de téléphoner. Ils m'ont dit qu'ils ont téléphoné plusieurs fois. Ils ont eu une panne[48]…

190

PAUL: Tout s'explique[49]!

[44] What do you know!
[45] as a matter of fact
[46] again
[47] after (at the end of)
[48] breakdown
[49] That explains everything!

CHALLENGE This reading includes some expressions, such as "Ça, par exemple!" that non-native speakers of French might not understand. "Mardi en huit" is another expression that gives the two American students some trouble. Can you think of any American expressions that you use in your daily life that non-native speakers of American English might not easily understand? **(Compare and Contrast)**

CHALLENGE
This feature asks you to expand upon what you have learned for enrichment.

Interlude *continued*

Vocabulaire de la lecture
Vocabulary practice follows
each reading, reinforcing
the *Mots clés* that appear
throughout the selection.
Words that appear in blue are
leçon vocabulary words in
Discovering French, Nouveau!

Vocabulaire de la lecture

Mots clés

un carnet d'adresses	*address book*	**goûter**	*to taste*
libre	*free*	**sourire**	*to smile*
prévenir	*to warn*	**sembler**	*to seem*
un tapis	*rug*	**étonné(e)**	*astonished, surprised*
une clé	*key*	**changer d'avis**	*to change one's mind*

A. Complétez chaque phrase par le mot clé qui convient *(fits)* le mieux.

1. Paul cherche le numéro de téléphone de Nathalie dans

   son _____.

2. Paul et David trouvent des _____ sous le _____
   pour ouvrir la porte.

3. Quand Nathalie voit les garçons, elle a l'air _____.

4. Paul et David peuvent accepter l'invitation de Nathalie parce

   qu'ils sont _____.

B. Mettez en regard *(Match)* le mot clé sur la gauche avec l'expression qui l'explique.

_____ **1.** prévenir   a. ce qu'on fait quand on est heureux

_____ **2.** sourire   b. ce qu'on fait quand on décide de faire
            quelque chose d'autre

_____ **3.** sembler   c. s'il y a beaucoup de choses à manger, on
            peut le faire au lieu de tout manger

_____ **4.** changer d'avis   d. avoir l'air de

_____ **5.** goûter   e. dire à quelqu'un ce qui va arriver

Tu as compris?

1. Qui est Paul et qui est David?

2. Quelle est la première surprise?

3. Quelle est la deuxième surprise?

4. Qu'est-ce qu'il y a pour le déjeuner?

5. Qui est la personne qui est entrée dans l'appartement?

6. Pourqoui est-ce que les garçons ne veulent pas manger le gâteau de Nathalie?

Connexion personnelle

If you were having out of town guests, what foods might you have on hand for them? Write a sample menu here.

Menu pour mes amis

Unité 3
Quatre surprises   33

Tu as compris?
Comprehension questions check your understanding and provide the opportunity to practice new vocabulary words.

Connexion personnelle
These short writing activities help you see connections between what happens in the selection and in your own life.

Lectures supplémentaires

Notes in the margins make literature from the French-speaking world accessible and help you read works by famous authors such as Apollinaire and Baudelaire.

Reading Strategy
This feature provides reading tips and strategies that help you effectively approach the material.

What You Need to Know
This section provides a key to help you unlock the selection so that you can understand and enjoy it.

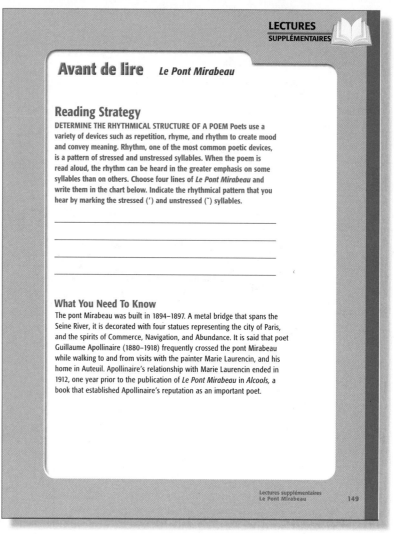

LECTURES
SUPPLÉMENTAIRES

Avant de lire   *Le Pont Mirabeau*

Reading Strategy

DETERMINE THE RHYTHMICAL STRUCTURE OF A POEM Poets use a variety of devices such as repetition, rhyme, and rhythm to create mood and convey meaning. Rhythm, one of the most common poetic devices, is a pattern of stressed and unstressed syllables. When the poem is read aloud, the rhythm can be heard in the greater emphasis on some syllables than on others. Choose four lines of *Le Pont Mirabeau* and write them in the chart below. Indicate the rhythmical pattern that you hear by marking the stressed (') and unstressed (˜) syllables.

_____

_____

_____

_____

What You Need To Know

The pont Mirabeau was built in 1894–1897. A metal bridge that spans the Seine River, it is decorated with four statues representing the city of Paris, and the spirits of Commerce, Navigation, and Abundance. It is said that poet Guillaume Apollinaire (1880–1918) frequently crossed the pont Mirabeau while walking to and from visits with the painter Marie Laurencin, and his home in Auteuil. Apollinaire's relationship with Marie Laurencin ended in 1912, one year prior to the publication of *Le Pont Mirabeau* in *Alcools*, a book that established Apollinaire's reputation as an important poet.

Lectures supplémentaires
Le Pont Mirabeau   149

LECTURES SUPPLÉMENTAIRES

À réfléchir...

1. Which of the following best expresses the main idea of the poem? **(Main Idea)**
   - ☐ Love lasts forever.
   - ☐ Love is best remembered on a bridge.
   - ☐ The happiest memories are those of love.
   - ☐ Time, like the river, passes on, but the painful memories of a love lost remain.

2. How does the two-line refrain enhance the meaning of the poem? **(Draw Conclusions)**

_____

_____

_____

▌▌À MARQUER⟩ ANALYSE LITTÉRAIRE You've learned that figurative language is language that means something other than its literal meaning. Read the poem and underline examples of figurative language. Write them here.

_____

_____

_____

READING TIP Sometimes poems do not observe standard writing conventions. Often, for example, each line of a poem starts with a capital letter, even though that line is not the beginning of a new sentence. Poets are free to establish their own style. Note that this poem has no punctuation.

150 Lectures pour tous

À propos de l'auteur

Guillaume Apollinaire–Wilhelm Apollinaris de Kostrowitsky–est né à Rome d'une mère polonaise et d'un père italien. Il a passé sa jeunesse en France sur la Côte d'Azur, et en 1889, il déménage à Paris où il passera le reste de sa vie sauf deux ans à l'étranger. Il est connu surtout comme poète lyrique mais il est également l'auteur de critiques d'art. Les plus grands sujets de sa poésie sont l'amour, la nostalgie de la jeunesse, et la solitude.

〰〰〰〰〰〰

Le Pont Mirabeau

Sous le pont Mirabeau **coule** la Seine
Et nos amours
Faut-il qu'il m'en **souvienne**
La joie venait toujours après **la peine**

5 Vienne la nuit sonne l'heure
Les jours s'en vont[1] je **demeure**

Les mains dans les mains restons **face à face**
Tandis que sous
Le pont de nos bras passe
10 Des éternels regards l'onde[2] si **lasse**

[1] go away   [2] waters

MOTS CLÉS

couler to flow
se souvenir de to remember
la peine sadness, hurt
demeurer to live (on); to stay

face à face face to face
tandis que while
las(se) weary

Discovering French, Nouveau! Level 2

À propos de l'auteur
Each literary selection begins with a short author biography that provides cultural context.

À réfléchir...
Point-of-use questions check your comprehension and ask you to think critically about the passage.

▌▌À MARQUER⟩ ANALYZE LITTÉRAIRE
This feature encourages you to focus on one aspect of literary analysis as you read.

Academic and Informational Reading

This section helps you read informational material and prepare for other classes and standardized tests.

VARIED TYPES OF READINGS

The wide variety of academic and informational selections helps you access different types of readings and develop specific techniques for those reading types.

Academic and Informational Reading

In this section you'll find strategies to help you read all kinds of informational materials. The examples here range from magazines you read for fun to textbooks to schedules. Applying these simple and effecive techniques will help you be a successful reader of the many texts you encounter every day.

155

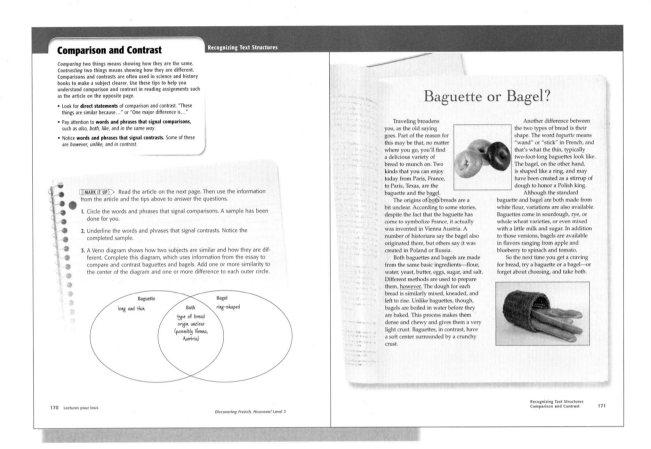

Comparison and Contrast

Comparing two things means showing how they are the same. *Contrasting* two things means showing how they are different. Comparisons and contrasts are often used in science and history books to make a subject clearer. Use these tips to help you understand comparison and contrast in reading assignments such as the article on the opposite page.

- Look for **direct statements** of comparison and contrast. "These things are similar because…" or "One major difference is…"
- Pay attention to **words and phrases that signal comparisons**, such as *also, both, like,* and *in the same way.*
- Notice **words and phrases that signal contrasts.** Some of these are *however, unlike,* and *in contrast.*

MARK IT UP Read the article on the next page. Then use the information from the article and the tips above to answer the questions.

1. Circle the words and phrases that signal comparisons. A sample has been done for you.

2. Underline the words and phrases that signal contrasts. Notice the completed sample.

3. A Venn diagram shows how two subjects are similar and how they are different. Complete this diagram, which uses information from the essay to compare and contrast baguettes and bagels. Add one or more similarity to the center of the diagram and one or more difference to each outer circle.

Baguette
long and thin

Both
type of bread
origin unclear
(possibly Vienna,
Austria)

Bagel
ring-shaped

Discovering French, Nouveau! Level 2

Baguette or Bagel?

Traveling broadens you, as the old saying goes. Part of the reason for this may be that, no matter where you go, you'll find a delicious variety of bread to munch on. Two kinds that you can enjoy today from Paris, France, to Paris, Texas, are the baguette and the bagel.

The origins of both breads are a bit unclear. According to some stories, despite the fact that the baguette has come to symbolize France, it actually was invented in Vienna Austria. A number of historians say the bagel also originated there, but others say it was created in Poland or Russia.

Both baguettes and bagels are made from the same basic ingredients—flour, water, yeast, butter, eggs, sugar, and salt. Different methods are used to prepare them, however. The dough for each bread is similarly mixed, kneaded, and left to rise. Unlike baguettes, though, bagels are boiled in water before they are baked. This process makes them dense and chewy and gives them a very light crust. Baguettes, in contrast, have a soft center surrounded by a crunchy crust.

Another difference between the two types of bread is their shape. The word *baguette* means "wand" or "stick" in French, and that's what the thin, typically two-foot-long baguettes look like. The bagel, on the other hand, is shaped like a ring, and may have been created as a stirrup of dough to honor a Polish king.

Although the standard baguette and bagel are both made from white flour, variations are also available. Baguettes come in sourdough, rye, or whole wheat varieties, or even mixed with a little milk and sugar. In addition to those versions, bagels are available in flavors ranging from apple and blueberry to spinach and tomato.

So the next time you get a craving for bread, try a baguette or a bagel—or forget about choosing, and take both.

SKILL DEVELOPMENT
These activities offer graphic organizers, Mark It Up features, and other reading support to help you comprehend and think critically about the selection.

Test Preparation for All Learners

Lectures pour tous offers models, strategies, and practice to help you prepare for standardized tests.

TEST PREPARATION STRATEGIES

- Successful test taking
- Reading test model and practice–long selections
- Reading test model and practice–short selections
- Functional reading test model and practice
- Revising-and-editing test model and practice
- Writing test model and practice
- Scoring rubrics

NOTES

READING STRATEGIES FOR ASSESSMENT

Note who the building was built for. How will this information help you understand the reputation of the Paris Opera House?

Pay attention to topic sentences. What new information will this paragraph tell you about the Paris Opera House?

Reading Test Model

SHORT SELECTIONS

DIRECTIONS Use the following to practice your skills. Read the paragraphs carefully. Then answer the multiple-choice questions that follow.

The Paris Opera House

The Paris Opera House, also known as the Opéra Garnier, Palais Garnier, and Théâtre Nationale de l'Opéra, was designed by Charles Garnier. He won a competition to design it in 1860. It was built during the Second Empire, between 1861 and 1875, for Napoleon III.

It is a remarkable building in several ways. In its heyday, it was a popular place for the members of the French aristocracy to gather. There was actually more space devoted to socializing than to its massive 118,000-square-foot stage. One favorite gathering place was the Grand Staircase, a model of which can be viewed at the Musée d'Orsay. The building was renowned for its opulence. Its main chandelier weighs six and half tons!

Today, the Opéra Garnier shows mostly ballet. More operas are shown at the new Opéra de la Bastille, a far larger and less well-regarded building.

Discovering French, Nouveau! Level 2

Revising-and-Editing Test Model

DIRECTIONS Read the following paragraph carefully. Then answer the multiple-choice questions that follow. After answering the questions, read the material in the side columns to check your answer strategies.

¹ Last summer my cousins and me visited Canada and we spent a morning in Old Quebec. ² We seen a brochure that said it would be 400 years old in 2008! ³ It was the center of New France during the 17th and 18th centuries. ⁴ It was known as the center of French culture. ⁵ In the Western Hemisphere. ⁶ Because of its history and architecture, UNESCO declared Old Quebec a World Heritage Site. ⁷ We would of stayed longer, but our bus was leaving for the return trip to Montreal. ⁸ We plan to go to Old Quebec again one day. ⁹ We plan to explore the city further.

1 Which of the following is the best way to rewrite the beginning of sentence 1?

   A. Last summer, us cousins…

   B. Last summer, my cousins and I…

   C. Last summer, me and my cousins…

   D. Last summer, I and my cousins…

2 What is the correct way to punctuate the two complete thoughts in sentence 1?

   A. …visited Canada: and we…

   B. …visited Canada; and we…

   C. …visited Canada, and we…

   D. …visited Canada–and we…

READING STRATEGIES FOR ASSESSMENT

Watch for common errors. Highlight or underline errors such as incorrect punctuation, spelling, or capitalization; fragments or run-on sentences; and missing or misplaced information.

ANSWER STRATEGIES

Personal Pronouns When deciding whether to use the personal pronoun *me* or *I* in a sentence, think about how the pronoun is used. If it's used as the subject, use *I*. If it's used as an object, use *me*.

Correct Punctuation Sentence 1 is a compound sentence. That is, it has two independent clauses joined by the conjunction *and*. In such cases, the correct punctuation is a comma.

Writing Test Model

DIRECTIONS Many tests ask you to write an essay in response to a writing prompt. A writing prompt is a brief statement that describes a writing situation. Some writing prompts ask you to explain *what*, *why*, or *how*. Others ask you to convince someone of something.

As you analyze the following writing prompts, read and respond to the notes in the side columns. Then look at the response to each prompt. The notes in the side columns will help you understand why each response is considered strong.

Prompt A

   Everyone enjoys leisure time and everyone has a favorite way to enjoy such time. Think about what you like to do most with your leisure time.

   Now write an essay that describes your favorite leisure activity. Include details that enable readers to understand and experience your enthusiasm.

Strong Response

   Between school and working at my family's hardware store, I don't have much time to myself. However, when I can grab a couple of hours of free time, I love jumping on my bike and riding the back roads just outside of Carpentersville. Whether I'm alone or with friends, a long ride helps clear my mind and refresh my spirit.

   I ride a road bike, a lightweight, sleek machine with a red pearl finish. Its drop handlebars, thin tires, and sixteen gears are perfect for propelling me along the gently rolling hills of these parts. I've devised several different routes through the countryside. Some are designed for speed—perfect for those days when I'm looking for a really good workout. Other routes are more scenic. I can take these

NOTES

ANALYZING THE PROMPT

Identify the topic. Read the first paragraph of the prompt carefully. Underline the topic of the essay you will write.

Understand what's expected of you. The second paragraph of the prompt explains what you must do and offers suggestions on how to create a successful response.

ANSWER STRATEGIES

Grab the reader's attention. This opening paragraph is an invitation to the reader to go riding with the writer and experience what he experiences on his bike.

Provide interesting information. Here the writer describes his bike and the routes he takes, painting a picture for the reader.

Avant de lire   *Le concert des Diplodocus*

Reading Strategy

PREDICT USING TITLES AND ART In order to get a sense of what a reading is going to be about, it's a good idea to look at some of the clues given to you: title, subheadings, illustrations, etc. For this reading, look at the title and study the headings and four cartoons. Try to predict what might happen in the reading. Write your prediction here.

_____

_____

_____

_____

_____

As you read, see how many of your guesses are correct.

What You Need To Know

France has a rich history of pop music, beginning in the fifties with the **chansonniers** (much like the American "crooners")—Maurice Chevalier, Jacques Brel, Georges Brassens, Yves Montand, and Edith Piaf. The music of the late fifties and early sixties was influenced by the American music scene—be-bop, rock and roll, and country—and turned out such French stars as Johnny Hallyday (the "French Elvis") and Serge Gainsbourg. In the 1960s, French female pop stars, who combined the best of British beat bands, American rock, and the French **chansonnier** tradition, exploded onto the scene and became known—after the term for the French youth scene of the sixties—as the **yé yé** girls. The most famous of these are Sylvie Vartan, France Gall, and Françoise Hardy.

Le concert des Diplodocus

SCÈNE 1
Chez les Lagrange: 7 heures et demie

DIS DONC, CATHERINE, OÙ VAS-TU?

JE VAIS CHEZ SUZANNE.

Les Lagrange viennent de dîner. Catherine, la fille aînée[1], met son manteau. Sa mère veut savoir où elle va ce soir.

— Dis donc, Catherine, où vas-tu?

5 — Je vais chez Suzanne.

— Chez Suzanne? Mais c'est la troisième fois que tu vas chez elle cette semaine. Qu'est-ce que tu vas faire là-bas?

— Euh… , je vais étudier avec elle. Nous
10 allons préparer ensemble[2] l'examen de maths.

— Dans ce cas, d'accord. Mais promets-moi de rentrer tôt à la maison.

— **Sois tranquille,** Maman. Je vais
15 revenir à onze heures.

[1] older   [2] together

MOTS CLÉS
être tranquille to relax, be calm

À réfléchir…

1. Number the following statements to show the order of events. (**Sequence of Events**)

_____ Catherine meets her boyfriend at the Café de l'Esplanade.

_____ Catherine's parents see her on T.V.

_____ Catherine and Jean-Michel arrive at the concert of Diplodocus.

_____ Catherine tells her parents she's going to her friend's house to study for math.

_____ Catherine decides never to lie to her parents.

2. Why do you think Catherine tells her parents she's going to Suzanne's house? (**Infer**)

_____

_____

À MARQUER GRAMMAIRE
You've learned to use the expressions **aller** + infinitive to say what someone is *going to do* as well as **venir de** + infinitive to say what someone *has just done*. In Scène 1, underline three examples of **aller** + infinitive. In Scène 2 and Scène 3, underline two examples of **venir** + infinitive.

READING TIP Look at the *Tu as compris?* questions before you begin reading. Then, read the selection with those questions in mind. Look for the answers as you read.

SCÈNE 2
Au Café de l'Esplanade: 8 heures

En réalité Catherine ne va pas chez Suzanne. Elle va au Café de l'Esplanade. Pourquoi va-t-elle là-bas? Parce que ce soir elle a **rendez-vous** avec son copain Jean-Michel.

20 Catherine arrive au café à huit heures. Jean-Michel est là depuis dix minutes.

— Salut, Catherine, ça va?

— Oui, ça va.

— Dis, j'ai une surprise!

25 — Ah bon? Quoi?

— Je viens d'acheter deux **billets** pour le concert des Diplodocus.

— Pour ce soir?

— Oui, pour ce soir. Tu viens?

30 — Euh… Je voudrais bien venir, mais… j'ai un problème.

Catherine explique la situation à Jean-Michel. Elle explique en particulier qu'elle doit être chez elle à onze heures.

35 — Ce n'est pas un problème. J'ai ma moto. Je vais te **ramener** chez toi après le concert.

MOTS CLÉS
avoir rendez-vous to have a date
un billet ticket

ramener to bring back, take home

—Bon, alors d'accord.

Et Catherine et Jean-Michel vont au concert sur
40 la moto de Jean-Michel.

SCÈNE 3

Au concert:
9 heures moins le quart

Ce soir les Diplodocus vont donner leur grand
concert de l'année. Il y a **beaucoup de monde**
dans **la salle.** Il y a aussi la télévision. Jean-
Michel et Catherine viennent d'arriver.
45 Une journaliste s'approche de[3] Catherine.

— Bonjour, mademoiselle, vous êtes une
fan des Diplodocus?

— Oui, ils sont super-cools! J'ai tous
leurs CD.

50 — Vous venez souvent ici?

— Non, je ne viens pas très souvent.
C'est la première fois que je viens cette
année.

— Merci, mademoiselle.

––––––
[3] comes over

MOTS CLÉS
beaucoup de monde   a lot of people   **la salle**   concert hall

55 Le concert commence. Tout le monde **crie**
et applaudit. C'est vraiment un concert
extraordinaire.

SCÈNE 4
Chez les Lagrange: 11 heures

Jean-Michel vient de raccompagner Catherine.
Catherine rentre chez elle. Elle regarde sa
60 montre. Ouf! Il est exactement onze heures.

Catherine va dans le salon. Ses parents sont
en train de regarder la télé. En exclusivité, il y
a justement[4] un reportage[5] sur le concert des
Diplodocus.

---

[4] at that moment   [5] news story

MOTS CLÉS
crier to shout, scream

65 — D'où viens-tu, Catherine?

— Euh… eh bien, je viens de chez Suzanne.

(En ce moment **apparaît** l'interview de Catherine.)

70 — Tiens, c'est curieux… Regarde cette fille. Tu ne trouves pas que vous vous ressemblez comme deux gouttes d'eau?

— Euh… c'est que…

— Inutile d'insister. La prochaine fois, 75 dis la vérité[6]. C'est plus simple.

Confuse[7], Catherine va dans sa chambre. Cette expérience lui a donné[8] une bonne leçon. C'est la première fois qu'elle a **menti** à ses parents.

80 C'est aussi la dernière.

---

[6] tell the truth   [7] ashamed
[8] gave her

ILS SE RESSEMBLENT COMME DEUX GOUTTES D'EAU.

MOTS CLÉS
apparaître to appear

mentir to lie

Unité 1
Le concert des Diplodocus   7

Vocabulaire de la lecture

Mots clés

être tranquille *to relax, be calm*

avoir rendez-vous *to have a date*

un billet *ticket*

ramener *to bring back, take home*

beaucoup de monde *a lot of people*

la salle *concert hall*

crier *to shout, scream*

apparaître *to appear*

mentir *to lie*

la fille *daughter*

A. Fill in each blank with the appropriate vocabulary word.

Catherine a _____ avec son copain Jean-Michel. Il a

acheté des _____ pour un concert des Diplodocus.

Au concert, il y a _____ dans la _____.

Catherine est la _____ aînée de la famille Lagrange.

B. Match the verb on the left with the phrase on the right that is the closest to it in meaning.

_____ **1.** être tranquille

_____ **2.** ramener

_____ **3.** apparaître

_____ **4.** mentir

_____ **5.** crier

a. inventer une histoire

b. rester calme

c. faire beaucoup de bruit

d. exister tout d'un coup *(suddenly)*

e. amener à la maison

Tu as compris?

1. Où va Catherine? Pourquoi?

_____

2. Quelle est la surprise de Jean-Michel?

_____

3. Avec qui est-ce que Catherine parle dans la salle de concert?

_____

4. Quelle est la réaction de ses parents quand ils regardent l'interview de Catherine à la télé?

_____

5. Qu'est-ce que Catherine décide?

_____

Connexion personnelle

Imagine that you are Catherine. What might you write in your journal after you have returned home from seeing Diplodocus in concert? Include some of your feelings from the evening out with Jean-Michel as well as your feelings about having deceived your parents.

Cher journal,

Je viens de rentrer d'un concert

des Diplodocus avec Jean-Michel...

Avant de lire *Camping de printemps*

Reading Strategy

FOLLOWING PLOT Use a chart to help you follow what happens in this story. Show the beginning, middle and end of the story. This story is broken up into different sections to help you.

Beginning	Middle	End

What You Need To Know

Normandy is a region of northwestern France, bordered in the north by the English Channel. It occupies five percent of all France's acreage and supports approximately five percent of its population. Home to farmland, apple orchards, and fishing ports, Normandy is noted for its seafood and dairy products—especially Camembert cheese. Normandy is a popular tourist destination, too, and includes the cities of Rouen and Caen, the ports of Le Havre and Honfleur, as well as Mont Saint-Michel and the famous D-Day beaches along the coast.

Camping
de printemps

A. Les préparatifs

Il a fait très froid ce printemps et Jean-Christophe n'a pas encore[1] eu l'occasion d'utiliser[2] la tente de camping qu'il a reçue[3] pour son anniversaire. Finalement, la semaine

5 dernière, la météo[4] a annoncé du beau temps pour toute la semaine. Jean-Christophe a donc[5] décidé de faire du camping ce week-end. Il a proposé à Vincent et à Thomas, deux copains de lycée, de venir avec lui. Les deux

10 garçons ont accepté avec plaisir l'invitation de Jean-Christophe. Oui, mais où aller?

JEAN-CHRISTOPHE: Allons en Normandie!

VINCENT: Bonne idée, c'est une région que je ne connais[6] pas très bien.

15

---

[1] not yet   [2] to use
[3] received   [4] weather report
[5] therefore   [6] know

À réfléchir...

1. Read the story and then decide if the following statements are **vrai** (true) or **faux** (false). **(Locate the Main Idea)**

Jean-Christophe wants to go camping because he is eager to use the tent he got for his birthday.
V   F

Jean-Christophe and his friends decide to go camping in Normandy because it's a day trip on their scooters.
V   F

The three friends have a restful weekend camping in Normandy.
V   F

The boys almost get run down by a bull.
V   F

The boys think it might be fun to camp in a military testing zone.
V   F

2. Why is Jean-Christophe satisfied with the camping trip? **(Clarify)**

A MARQUER ▷ **GRAMMAIRE**

Look at the boxed paragraphs on pages 12 and 17. Underline all the forms of the **passé composé** and write them in the space below. Next to each verb, write its infinitive.

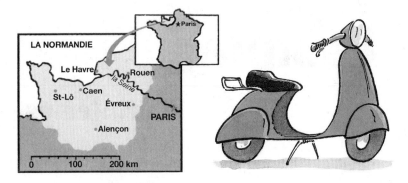

THOMAS: Et ce n'est pas très loin, c'est seulement[7] à 200 kilomètres d'ici. Avec nos scooters, on peut faire ça dans la journée.

20

JEAN-CHRISTOPHE: Bon, puisque[8] vous êtes d'accord, je vais préparer l'itinéraire. Rendez-vous samedi matin chez moi à huit heures. D'accord?

25

VINCENT: D'accord!

THOMAS: D'accord, et à samedi.

Vendredi soir après le dîner, Jean-Christophe
30 a pris une carte[9] et il a choisi un itinéraire qu'il a marqué au crayon rouge. Ensuite, il est allé dans sa chambre et il a choisi quelques vêtements qu'il a mis dans un grand sac avec sa tente. Puis, il est allé au garage et il a mis le
35 sac sur le porte-bagages[10] de son scooter. Tout est maintenant prêt[11] pour le départ.

---

[7] only   [8] since   [9] map
[10] baggage compartment   [11] ready

B. Une longue journée

Samedi matin à huit heures, Vincent et Thomas sont arrivés en scooter chez Jean-Christophe. Jean-Christophe a mis son casque. Il est monté sur[12] son scooter et les trois garçons sont partis en direction de la Normandie…

À midi, ils se sont arrêtés[13] et ils ont fait un pique-nique, puis ils sont remontés sur leurs scooters et ils ont continué leur route. En fin d'[14]après-midi, ils sont arrivés en Normandie. Vers[15] six heures, Jean-Christophe a donné le signal de l'arrêt.

JEAN-CHRISTOPHE: On s'arrête ici pour la nuit?

VINCENT: Oui, je suis fatigué[16].

THOMAS: Moi aussi. Où est-ce qu'on va camper?

Jean-Christophe a regardé la carte.

JEAN-CHRISTOPHE: Il y a une rivière près d'ici. Ça vous va?

VINCENT: Oui, bien sûr.

THOMAS: Allons-y.

Quelques minutes plus tard, les garçons sont arrivés au bord de[17] la rivière.

[12] got on [13] stopped
[14] at the end of [15] around
[16] tired [17] at the edge of

READING TIP Imagine, or visualize, what the story describes. Don't let unfamiliar words slow you down. Try to focus on the images and the descriptions.

READER'S SUCCESS STRATEGY You may have noticed that in French, as in English, certain words are related: they belong to the same word family. For instance,

une soirée (*evening*) is related to **un soir**

la fin (*end*) is related to **finir**

en vitesse (*very quickly*) is related to **vite**

Often you will discover the meaning of a word or expression you have not seen before if you can relate it to a word you already know. Can you guess the meanings of these words from the story? What words that you recognize are they related to?

le porte-bagages

la journée

Ils sont descendus de leurs scooters et ils ont commencé à préparer le terrain pour la nuit. Malheureusement, ce n'est pas l'endroit idéal pour camper.

65 THOMAS: Zut! **Un moustique!**

VINCENT: Aïe! Moi aussi, je me suis fait piquer[18] par un moustique.

JEAN-CHRISTOPHE: Aïe! Et moi aussi!

70 VINCENT: C'est la rivière qui attire[19] ces sales bêtes[20] … Si nous restons ici, nous allons être dévorés[21].

75 JEAN-CHRISTOPHE: Tu as raison. Allons un peu plus loin.

C. Un endroit tranquille

Jean-Christophe et ses deux copains ont pris leur matériel de camping et ils sont remontés sur leurs scooters. Quelques kilomètres
80 plus loin, ils ont trouvé une prairie isolée[22] et ils ont décidé de s'arrêter là pour la nuit. Jean-Christophe et Thomas ont commencé à monter[23] la tente. Vincent est allé chercher du bois[24] pour faire **un feu.** Il est vite revenu avec
85 une nouvelle[25] pour ses copains.

[18] I got stung	[19] attracts	[20] nasty bugs	[21] eaten up
[22] isolated	[23] to put up, pitch	[24] some wood	[25] news

MOTS CLÉS
un moustique mosquito
un feu fire
Discovering French, Nouveau! Level 2

VINCENT: Regardez, il y a une vache là-bas.

JEAN-CHRISTOPHE: Ce n'est pas une vache. C'est un taureau[26].

90 THOMAS: Est-ce qu'il est dangereux?

JEAN-CHRISTOPHE: Euh… je ne sais pas.

Brusquement, le taureau s'est mis à[27] courir[28] dans la direction des garçons.

95 VINCENT: Il n'a pas l'air très content.

THOMAS: C'est vrai! Il n'est certainement pas très heureux qu'on occupe son territoire.

100

VINCENT: On reste ici?

JEAN-CHRISTOPHE: Non, il vaut mieux[29] partir!

Et, à nouveau[30], les trois garçons ont pris leur
105 matériel et ils sont repartis. Finalement, à huit heures, ils sont arrivés près d'une forêt.

THOMAS: Ici, au moins[31], il n'y a pas de taureau furieux.

VINCENT: Et pas de moustiques.

110 JEAN-CHRISTOPHE: Alors, c'est ici que nous allons camper.

Jean-Christophe a vite installé la tente. Vincent a allumé[32] un feu et Thomas a préparé un excellent dîner. **Tout le monde** a mangé

| [26] bull | [27] began to | [28] run | [29] it is better |
| [30] again | [31] at least | [32] lit | |

MOTS CLÉS
tout le monde   everyone

¹¹⁵ avec appétit. Après le dîner, Vincent a pris
sa guitare et ses copains ont chanté avec lui.
Enfin, à dix heures et demie, les trois garçons
sont allés dans la tente, heureux d'avoir
trouvé un endroit si tranquille pour passer
¹²⁰ la nuit.

D. Une nuit mouvementée

Cette nuit-là, Vincent n'a pas très bien dormi.
Vers trois heures du matin, il est sorti de la
tente pour prendre l'air. Soudain, il a vu une
lueur³³ bleue dans le ciel³⁴… Puis une lueur
¹²⁵ rouge… Puis une lueur verte… Il est rentré
dans la tente pour alerter ses copains.

VINCENT: Dites, les gars³⁵, je
viens de voir quelque
chose d'extraordinaire.

¹³⁰ JEAN-CHRISTOPHE: Quoi?

³³ flash of light   ³⁴ sky   ³⁵ guys

VINCENT: Il y a des lueurs dans le ciel.

THOMAS: Mais, mon pauvre vieux, ce sont des **éclairs.**

135

VINCENT: Des éclairs? Tu as déjà vu des éclairs bleus, rouges et verts, toi?

JEAN-CHRISTOPHE: Tu as **rêvé!**

140 Tout à coup[36], des explosions ont interrompu le silence de la nuit. Bang! Poum! Bang! Bang! Poum!

> Jean-Christophe a ouvert[37] la tente. Il a entendu des **bruits** étranges, puis des voix
> 145 humaines très près. Bientôt[38] une douzaine d'hommes armés ont encerclé la tente. Les garçons sont sortis de la tente en vitesse[39].
> Le chef de la bande d'hommes a demandé à Jean-Christophe:

150

LE CHEF: Qu'est-ce que vous faites ici?

JEAN-CHRISTOPHE: Euh, eh bien, nous faisons du camping.

LE CHEF: Du camping?

155 Mais vous êtes complètement fous[40]. Vous voulez mourir[41]?

JEAN-CHRISTOPHE: (tremblant) Euh, non, pourquoi?

---

[36] suddenly   [37] opened
[38] soon   [39] very quickly
[40] crazy   [41] to die

MOTS CLÉS
un éclair (flash of) lightning   **un bruit** noise
rêver to dream

CHALLENGE How do you think Jean-Christophe might do things differently the next time he plans a camping trip? **(Draw Conclusions)**

160   LE CHEF: Comment? Vous n'avez pas vu la pancarte⁴² quand vous êtes entrés dans cette forêt?

JEAN-CHRISTOPHE: Euh, non.

165   LE CHEF: Regardez-la quand vous partirez⁴³. Et maintenant, décampez⁴⁴ en vitesse.

Les trois garçons ont vite **démonté** la tente,
170 puis ils ont quitté les lieux⁴⁵ précipitamment⁴⁶. Quand ils sont sortis de la forêt, ils ont vu une énorme pancarte avec cette inscription:

DANGER
TERRAIN MILITAIRE
MANOEUVRES DE PRINTEMPS
DÉFENSE ABSOLUE D'ENTRER⁴⁷

Dimanche soir, Jean-Christophe est rentré chez lui, fatigué, mais content
175 d'avoir utilisé sa tente.

---

⁴² sign	⁴³ will leave	⁴⁴ break camp and leave
⁴⁵ left the place	⁴⁶ very quickly	⁴⁷ absolutely no trespassing

MOTS CLÉS
   démonter   to take down

Vocabulaire de la lecture

Mots clés

un **moustique**   *mosquito*
un **feu**   *fire*
tout le monde   *everyone*
un **éclair**   *(flash of) lightning*
rêver   *to dream*

un **bruit**   *noise*
démonter   *to take down*
la **rivière**   *river*
une **vache**   *cow*
une **forêt**   *forest*

A. Fill in each blank with the appropriate vocabulary word.

1. En été, c'est difficile d'être dehors pendant la nuit parce qu'il y a beaucoup

   de _____.

2. Quand on fait du camping, c'est bien de faire un _____ pour
   faire la cuisine.

3. Pendant les orages, il y a souvent les _____ dans le ciel.

4. Le matin, il faut _____ la tente.

B. Match the word on the left with the phrase on the right that is closest to it
in meaning.

_____ **1.** tout le monde

_____ **2.** un bruit

_____ **3.** une vache

_____ **4.** rêver

_____ **5.** la rivière

a. ce qu'on fait pendant qu'on dort

b. plus grand qu'un lac, mais plus petit
   qu'un océan

c. beaucoup de gens

d. un animal qui peut donner du lait ou
   du boeuf

e. quelque chose qu'on peut entendre

Tu as compris?

1. Pourquoi est-ce que Jean-Christophe veut faire du camping?

_____

2. Où est-ce que les trois garçons ont l'intention d'aller? Est-ce loin?

_____

3. Comment est-ce qu'ils vont voyager?

_____

4. Pourquoi est-ce que le bord de la rivière n'est pas l'endroit idéal?

_____

5. Pourquoi les garçons n'ont pas fait du camping dans la prairie isolée?

_____

Connexion personnelle

Make a list of all the qualities you would want to have in an ideal camping spot.

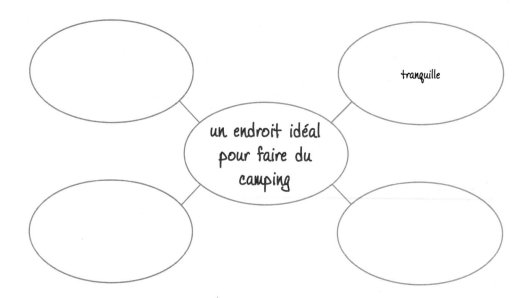

Avant de lire *Quatre surprises*

Reading Strategy

COMBINE STRATEGIES Put together the reading strategies you have practiced.

1. Look at the title and subtitles to predict the reading's theme.
2. Skim the reading to get a general idea of the content.
3. Use context clues to help you make intelligent guesses about new words.

Predict	Theme:
Skim	General Idea:
Use Context Clues	New Words:

What You Need To Know

Most inhabitants of Paris live in apartments. The typical apartment building has a **concierge** who lives on the ground floor, called the **rez-de-chaussée.** The **concierge** keeps the common areas clean and generally watches over the comings and goings of the residents. Most Paris apartment buildings also include an extra floor above the usual residences. This upper floor includes rooms that come with some of the more expensive apartments— rooms that are often converted to student rooms, or **chambres d'étudiants.** These rooms are also known as **chambres de bonnes,** or maids' rooms.

1. What mistakes do Paul and David make? Check two. **(Summarize)**

☐ They didn't bring a hostess gift to Nathalie.

☐ They had written down the wrong street address.

☐ They arrived on the wrong day.

☐ They didn't introduce themselves to Nathalie's aunt.

☐ They entered the wrong apartment.

2. How would you characterize the type of reception the two Americans received in Paris? **(Infer)**

_____

_____

_____

_____

▊▊À MARQUER ◆ GRAMMAIRE

In this unit, you've learned about the various uses of the definite, indefinite, and partitive articles. Look at the boxed sections of the text and note the various examples of how all three are used. Underline an example of each and write them here:

Definite Article:

_____

Indefinite Article:

_____

Partitive Article:

_____

Quatre surprises

L'invitation

Paul et David sont deux étudiants américains. Avec l'argent qu'ils ont économisé cette année, ils ont décidé de passer un mois en France. Ils viennent d'arriver à Paris.
5 Malheureusement, ils n'ont pas d'amis français.

> PAUL: Tu connais des gens à Paris?
>
> DAVID: Non, je ne connais personne. Et toi?
>
> 10 PAUL: Moi non plus. Attends, si! Ma soeur Christine a une correspondante¹ française qui habite à Paris. Je crois² que j'ai son nom dans mon **carnet d'adresses.**
> 15

Paul regarde dans son carnet d'adresses.

> PAUL: Voilà. La copine de ma soeur s'appelle Nathalie Descroix. J'ai son numéro de
> 20 téléphone...
>
> DAVID: Eh bien, téléphone-lui!

¹pen pal   ²believe, think

MOTS CLÉS
un carnet d'adresses address book

PAUL: Bon, d'accord. Je vais lui téléphoner.

Paul compose[3] le numéro de Nathalie.
25 Celle-ci[4] répond. Paul explique[5] qu'il est le frère de Christine et qu'il est à Paris avec un copain. Nathalie propose d'inviter les deux garçons à déjeuner.

NATHALIE: Tu es **libre** mardi en huit[6]?

30 Paul: Oui, bien sûr.

NATHALIE: Est-ce que tu veux déjeuner chez moi avec ton copain?

PAUL: Avec grand plaisir. Où est-ce que tu habites?

35 NATHALIE: J'habite une modeste chambre d'étudiante au 125, rue de Sèvres.

PAUL: À quel étage[7]?

NATHALIE: Au sixième étage. Donc, je
40 vous attends[8] mardi en huit à midi. Mais je vous **préviens,** ce sera[9] un repas très simple.

PAUL: Merci beaucoup pour ton invitation. À bientôt.

45 NATHALIE: Au revoir, à bientôt.

Dans son carnet, Paul note la date du 8 juillet.

[3] dials	[4] the latter (= Nathalie)
[5] explains	[6] a week from Tuesday
[7] floor	[8] I'm expecting you
[9] will be	

MOTS CLÉS
libre free   **prévenir** to warn

Première surprise

Le 8 juillet, Paul et David ont mis leurs plus beaux vêtements. Ils ont acheté un gros bouquet de fleurs et il sont allés chez Nathalie.

50 Arrivé devant l'immeuble[10] du 125, rue de Sèvres, Paul a regardé son carnet. «Nathalie habite au sixième étage.» Paul et David sont entrés dans l'immeuble. Puis ils ont monté les escaliers[11] et compté[12] les étages. «Deux, trois,
55 quatre, cinq, six.»

PAUL: Nous sommes au sixième étage.

DAVID: Et voilà la chambre de Nathalie.

60 Sur une porte, il y a en effet[13] une carte avec le nom: DESCROIX.

Paul a sonné[14]. Pas de réponse.

Il a sonné deux fois[15], trois fois, quatre fois… Toujours pas de réponse.

65 DAVID: Tu es sûr que Nathalie habite ici?

PAUL: Mais oui. Son nom est inscrit[16] sur la porte.

DAVID: Regarde, il y a une enveloppe
70 sous le **tapis.**

PAUL: C'est sûrement pour nous.

[10] (apartment) building   [11] stairs
[12] counted   [13] in fact
[14] rang the bell   [15] times
[16] written

MOTS CLÉS
un tapis rug

Paul a ouvert[17] l'enveloppe. Il a trouvé[18] des **clés** avec la note suivante[19]:

Chers amis,

Excusez-moi si je ne suis pas ici pour vous acueillir[20]. Ce matin, j'ai dû aller à l'hôpital rendre visite à une amie qui a eu un accident. Ce n'est pas grave, mais je ne serai pas de retour[21] avant trois heures. Entrez chez moi et faites comme chez vous. Le déjeuner est préparé. Ne m'attendez pas.

À bientôt,

N.D.

Deuxième surprise

Paul a pris les clés et il a ouvert la porte.

75 Une autre surprise attend les deux garçons. En effet, ce n'est pas dans «une modeste chambre d'étudiante» qu'ils sont entrés, mais dans un appartement relativement petit, mais très moderne et très confortable.

---

[17] opened   [18] found
[19] following   [20] to welcome you
[21] I won't be back

MOTS CLÉS
une clé key

80 Et sur la table de la salle à manger est servi un magnifique repas froid. Il y a du saumon fumé[22], du poulet rôti[23] avec de la mayonnaise, une salade, un grand nombre de fromages différents et, comme dessert, un énorme

85 gâteau au chocolat.

DAVID: Nathalie a parlé d'un repas très simple, mais en réalité, elle a préparé un véritable festin[24].

90 PAUL: C'est vrai. Nous allons nous régaler[25]!

DAVID: On commence[26]?

PAUL: Non! Attendons Nathalie. C'est plus poli.

95 DAVID: Tu as raison. Attendons-la!

Paul et David ont attendu, mais il est maintenant une heure et Nathalie n'est toujours pas là.

DAVID: J'ai faim.

100 PAUL: Moi aussi, j'ai une faim de loup[27].

DAVID: Alors, déjeunons! Après tout, Nathalie a dit de ne pas attendre.

105 Les garçons ont pris plusieurs[28] tranches[29] de saumon fumé. «Hm, c'est délicieux.» Puis, ils ont mangé du poulet rôti. «Fameux[30] aussi!»

---

[22] smoked salmon   [23] roasted
[24] real feast   [25] We're going to enjoy a delicious meal!
[26] begin   [27] I'm as hungry as a wolf
[28] several   [29] slices
[30] great

Puis ils ont pris de la salade et ils ont **goûté** à tous les fromages. Finalement, ils sont arrivés
110 au dessert. Ils ont pris un premier morceau de gâteau au chocolat, puis un deuxième, puis un autre et encore[31] un autre… Bientôt, ils ont fini tout le gâteau.

DAVID: Quel repas merveilleux!
115 Nathalie est une excellente cuisinière[32].

PAUL: C'est vrai… Mais, euh, maintenant je suis fatigué.

DAVID: Euh, moi aussi…

120 Paul et David ont quitté la table. Ils se sont assis[33] sur le sofa. Quelques minutes plus tard, ils sont complètement endormis[34].

Pendant qu'ils dormaient[35] le téléphone a sonné plusieurs fois. Dring, dring, dring,
125 dring, dring… Mais personne n'a répondu.

Troisième surprise

Il est maintenant trois heures. Quelqu'un est entré dans l'appartement. Paul et David se sont réveillés[36].

DAVID: Tiens, voilà Nathalie.
130 PAUL: Bonjour, Nathalie.

Mais la personne qui est entrée n'est pas Nathalie. C'est une dame d'une cinquantaine d'années[37], très élégante. Elle a l'air très surprise.

---

[31] still   [32] cook   [33] sat down
[34] asleep   [35] were sleeping   [36] woke up
[37] about fifty years old

MOTS CLÉS
goûter to taste

LA DAME: Qu'est-ce que vous faites ici?

135 Paul et David, à leur tour[38], sont très surpris.

PAUL: Nous attendons notre amie Nathalie.

LA DAME: Votre amie Nathalie n'habite pas ici.

140 DAVID: Mais alors, chez qui sommes-nous?

LA DAME: Vous êtes chez moi.

PAUL: Mais alors, qui êtes-vous?

Maintenant la dame **sourit.**

145 LA DAME: Je suis la tante de Nathalie et vous, vous êtes certainement ses amis. À votre accent, je vois que vous êtes américains. Elle m'a parlé de vous.

150 PAUL: Oh, excusez-nous, madame. Nathalie s'est trompée[39] quand elle nous a donné son adresse. Elle a dit qu'elle habitait[40] au sixième étage.

155 La dame **semble** s'amuser[41].

LA DAME: Mais non, elle ne s'est pas trompée. Nathalie habite bien[42] une chambre d'étudiante au sixième, l'étage au-dessus[43].
160 C'est vous qui vous êtes trompés! Vous êtes ici au cinquième étage.

---

[38] in turn [39] made a mistake [40] lived
[41] to be amused [42] indeed [43] above

MOTS CLÉS
sourire to smile   **sembler** to seem

Discovering French, Nouveau! Level 2

DAVID: Au cinquième étage? Je ne comprends pas! Nous avons compté les étages.

LA DAME: Votre erreur est bien excusable. Notre premier étage en France correspond au deuxième étage américain. Ainsi, vous avez pensé être au sixième étage. En réalité, vous êtes seulement au cinquième.

PAUL: Ça, par exemple[44]!

DAVID: Et le repas?

LA DAME: Je l'ai préparé pour des amis qui viennent passer la journée à Paris.

PAUL: Et la note sous le tapis?

LA DAME: Je l'ai écrite pour dire à mes amis que… Mais, au fait[45], où sont-ils?

Le téléphone sonne à nouveau[46]. La dame va répondre. Elle revient au bout[47] de quelques minutes.

LA DAME: Ce sont justement mes amis qui viennent de téléphoner. Ils m'ont dit qu'ils ont téléphoné plusieurs fois. Ils ont eu une panne[48]…

PAUL: Tout s'explique[49]!

---

[44] What do you know! [45] as a matter of fact
[46] again [47] after (at the end of)
[48] breakdown [49] That explains everything!

LA DAME: Pour vous et pour moi, mais pas pour Nathalie. Ma nièce vous attend certainement. Allez vite chez elle!

Quatrième et dernière surprise

195 Paul et David sont montés à l'étage supérieur[50]. Ils ont sonné à l'appartement de Nathalie. Celle-ci a ouvert la porte.

PAUL: Bonjour! Nathalie?

Nathalie a l'air **étonnée.**

200 NATHALIE: Oui, c'est moi. Et vous, vous êtes…?

PAUL: Je suis Paul. Et voici mon copain David.

NATHALIE: Ah, enchantée! Quelle bonne
205 surprise!

Paul, à son tour, est très étonné de l'air surpris de Nathalie.

PAUL: Euh… nous nous excusons de[51]…

210 NATHALIE: Ne vous excusez pas. Je suis très contente de vous voir. Vous avez de la chance car[52] j'avais l'intention d'aller au cinéma cet après-midi.

---

[50] higher   [51] we're sorry to
[52] car = parce que

MOTS CLÉS
étonné(e) astonished, surprised

215   PAUL: Au cinéma? Et l'invitation à
                      déjeuner?

      NATHALIE: Quel déjeuner?… Ah, oui.
                      J'espère que vous n'avez pas
                      changé d'avis. Je compte

220   absolument sur vous mardi
                      prochain.

        DAVID: Comment? Ce n'est pas pour
                      aujourd'hui?

         PAUL: Tu as dit «mardi huit». Nous

225   sommes bien le 8 juillet
                      aujourd'hui!

      NATHALIE: Non, j'ai dit «mardi en huit».
                      C'est différent. «Mardi en
                      huit» signifie[53] le mardi de la

230   semaine prochaine. Mais au
                      fait, vous avez probablement
                      faim. Malheureusement, je n'ai
                      rien préparé. Ah, si, attendez.
                      J'ai un gâteau au chocolat. Je

235   vais le chercher[54].

        DAVID: Euh, non merci. Pas
                      aujourd'hui.

      NATHALIE: Comment? Vous n'aimez pas
                      le gâteau au chocolat?

240   DAVID: Si, mais…

---

[53] means   [54] I'll go get it.

MOTS CLÉS
changer d'avis   to change one's mind

Vocabulaire de la lecture

Mots clés

un carnet d'adresses *address book*

libre *free*

prévenir *to warn*

un tapis *rug*

une clé *key*

goûter *to taste*

sourire *to smile*

sembler *to seem*

étonné(e) *astonished, surprised*

changer d'avis *to change one's mind*

A. Complétez chaque phrase par le mot clé qui convient *(fits)* le mieux.

1. Paul cherche le numéro de téléphone de Nathalie dans

   son _____.

2. Paul et David trouvent des _____ sous le _____
   pour ouvrir la porte.

3. Quand Nathalie voit les garçons, elle a l'air _____.

4. Paul et David peuvent accepter l'invitation de Nathalie parce

   qu'ils sont _____.

B. Mettez en regard *(Match)* le mot clé sur la gauche avec l'expression qui l'explique.

_____ **1.** prévenir

_____ **2.** sourire

_____ **3.** sembler

_____ **4.** changer d'avis

_____ **5.** goûter

a. ce qu'on fait quand on est heureux

b. ce qu'on fait quand on décide de faire
   quelque chose d'autre

c. s'il y a beaucoup de choses à manger, on
   peut le faire au lieu de tout manger

d. avoir l'air de

e. dire à quelqu'un ce qui va arriver

Tu as compris?

1. Qui est Paul et qui est David?

_____

2. Quelle est la première surprise?

_____

3. Quelle est la deuxième surprise?

_____

_____

4. Qu'est-ce qu'il y a pour le déjeuner?

_____

_____

5. Qui est la personne qui est entrée dans l'appartement?

_____

6. Pourqoui est-ce que les garçons ne veulent pas manger le gâteau de Nathalie?

_____

Connexion personnelle

If you were having out of town guests, what foods might you have on hand for them? Write a sample menu here.

Menu pour mes amis

Avant de lire   *Un Américain à Paris*

Reading Strategy

CATEGORIZE DETAILS Sometimes small cultural misunderstandings can get in the way of our enjoyment of life in a foreign country. Skim the reading and then mark in the chart below which features of daily life give Harry Hapless difficulty.

	Oui	Non
les heures d'ouverture de la banque		
les fêtes nationales		
la nourriture		
l'heure officielle		
les pourboires		

What You Need To Know

In many ways, daily life in France and daily life in the United States are similar. But there are some important differences that might confuse a tourist who is unfamiliar with French customs. One obvious difference between France and the United States regards our two systems of measurement. France, like most countries besides the United States, uses the metric system.

Tipping is handled differently in each country. In France, the tip is usually included in the price of a service or meal (when it is included in your restaurant bill, you will generally see a note that says **service compris).**

France and the United States share many of the same holidays, but France also celebrates many Catholic feast days as **jours fériés**—official holidays when schools and businesses are closed.

Un Américain
~ À Paris ~

À réfléchir...
What kinds of differences
might you expect to discover
during a trip to a foreign
country? **(Extend)**

Allez-vous visiter la France un jour? Si vous allez en France, vous observerez[1] certaines différences entre **la vie quotidienne** en France et aux États-Unis.

5 Ces différences ne sont pas très importantes, mais elles existent tout de même[2]. Et parfois, elles sont la source de petits problèmes.

Voici certains problèmes qui sont arrivés à Harry Hapless, un touriste américain qui ne

10 connaît pas très bien les **habitudes** françaises. Pouvez-vous expliquer[3] la cause de ces problèmes?

---

[1] will observe   [2] all the same, nevertheless   [3] explain

MOTS CLÉS
  la vie quotidienne daily life   **une habitude** a custom, habit

1 Harry Hapless arrive en France le 30 avril au soir. Il prend un taxi et va directement à
15 son hôtel. **Le lendemain** matin, qui est un mercredi, Harry dit: «J'ai besoin d'argent. Je vais aller changer des dollars à la banque.» La première banque où il va est fermée[4]. La deuxième et la troisième aussi.
20 En fait[5], toutes les banques sont fermées ce matin. Pourquoi?

• En France, les banques sont ouvertes seulement[6] l'après-midi.

• En France, les banques sont fermées le
25 mercredi.

• En France, le premier mai est **un jour férié.**

Interprétation

En France, le premier mai est un jour férié.

En France et dans beaucoup d'autres pays, le premier mai est la fête du Travail.
30 Évidemment, on ne travaille pas ce jour-là. Les magasins, les bureaux et les banques sont fermés. (Aux États-Unis, la fête du Travail est le premier lundi de septembre.)

2 Un soir, Harry Hapless va au restaurant
35 et commande un steak-frites. Le service est **lent.** Le steak est dur[7]. Les frites sont froides. Le serveur n'est pas poli… Et l'addition est très chère: 30 euros! Pour

---

[4] closed   [5] in fact   [6] only   [7] tough

MOTS CLÉS
le lendemain the next day   **lent** slow
un jour férié a holiday

Discovering French, Nouveau! Level 2

montrer son mécontentement[8], Harry

40 laisse un petit pourboire: deux euros seulement. L'attitude du serveur change. Il est maintenant très aimable avec Harry. Pourquoi?

- Le serveur a des remords[9].
45 - Le serveur aime les touristes américains.
- En France, le pourboire[10] est compris[11] dans l'addition.

Interprétation

En France, le pourboire est compris dans l'addition. Puisque le service de 15% (quinze pour 50 cent) est compris dans l'addition, en général on laisse seulement quelques petites pièces de monnaie au serveur.

3 Un jour, Harry Hapless est invité à dîner chez Jacques Lachance, son copain 55 d'université. Harry, qui est un homme poli, veut apporter un cadeau[12] à Madame Lachance, la femme de son copain. Oui, mais quoi? Harry sait que les Françaises aiment beaucoup les fleurs. Il passe chez 60 une marchande de fleurs. Il regarde les roses, les tulipes, les bégonias, les géraniums… Finalement il choisit un **énorme** pot de chrysanthèmes. La marchande prend le pot, l' enveloppe 65 dans du joli papier, décore le paquet[13]

NOTES

À MARQUER GRAMMAIRE
You've been learning how to use direct and indirect object pronouns. In Section 3, circle the examples of direct and indirect object pronouns that you find.

---

[8] displeasure [9] regrets, remorse [10] tip
[11] included [12] gift, present [13] package

MOTS CLÉS
énorme large, enormous

Sometimes you can guess the meaning of a new French word because it looks like an English word that you know. For example, in Section 4, you encountered the phrase: *Harry monte les escaliers.* **Escaliers** might have reminded you of the English word *escalator,* and you might have figured out that Harry was climbing the stairs. Look at the following words and see if you can figure out what they mean. Write down the English word that they ressemble.

1. **une marchande** de fleurs

ENGLISH WORD	MEANING

2. Madame Lachance a l'air **consternée.**

ENGLISH WORD	MEANING

3. C'est au cinquième étage, mais **l'ascenseur** ne marche pas.

ENGLISH WORD	MEANING

avec un ruban[14] et le donne à Harry. Très content de son achat, Harry arrive chez les Lachance. Il sonne[15]. Son ami Jacques lui ouvre[16] la porte. Harry entre et présente
70 son cadeau à Madame Lachance. Celle-ci[17] le prend et remercie[18] Harry profusément … Mais quand elle ouvre le paquet, elle a l'air consternée. Pourquoi?

- Madame Lachance est allergique aux
75 fleurs.

- En France, les chrysanthèmes sont un signe de grand amour[19].

- En France, les chrysanthèmes sont un signe de **deuil.**

Interprétation

80 *En France, les chrysanthèmes sont un signe de deuil.*
Le premier novembre, qui est la fête de la Toussaint[20], les Français honorent leurs défunts[21]. Traditionnellement on va au cimetière[22] et on met des pots de
85 chrysanthèmes sur la tombe des gens de sa famille.

4 Harry Hapless a mal aux dents[23]. Il a rendez-vous[24] chez un dentiste qui habite dans un immeuble[25] ancien. Arrivé
90 dans cet immeuble, Harry demande à la concierge[26] à quel étage[27] habite le dentiste.

[14] ribbon	[15] rings (the doorbell)	[16] opens	[17] the latter
[18] thanks	[19] love	[20] All Saints' Day	[21] dead
[22] cemetery	[23] has a toothache	[24] an appointment	
[25] building	[26] building superintendent	[27] floor (of a building)	

MOTS CLÉS
le deuil mourning

95 La concierge lui répond: «Le docteur Ledentu? C'est au cinquième étage, mais aujourd'hui l'ascenseur ne marche pas[28].» Harry dit: «Ça ne fait rien[29], je vais monter à pied.» Harry monte les escaliers et compte les étages: deux, trois, quatre, cinq. «Je suis au cinquième étage», dit Harry, et il sonne. Un homme en blanc

100 ouvre la porte. Ce n'est pas un dentiste mais un peintre[30]. Harry lui explique qu'il a rendez-vous avec le docteur Ledentu. Le peintre lui répond: «Je ne connais pas le docteur Ledentu. Ici, c'est chez Madame

105 Masson. Je repeins son appartement. Allez voir la concierge.»

Quel est le problème?

- Harry s'est trompé[31] d'étage.
- La concierge a donné un mauvais[32]
110 renseignement[33] à Harry.
- Ce jour-là, le docteur Ledentu s'est déguisé[34] en peintre.

Interprétation

Harry s'est trompé d'étage.

Il y a une différence d'un étage entre les
115 étages français et américains. Voici la correspondance entre ces étages:

ÉTAGES FRANÇAIS	ÉTAGES AMÉRICAINS
rez-de-chaussée	*first floor*
premier étage	*second (not first) floor*
120 **deuxième étage**	*third (not second) floor*
dix-neuvième étage	*twentieth (not nineteenth) floor*

---

[28] isn't working [29] that doesn't matter [30] painter
[31] made a mistake [32] wrong [33] information
[34] disguised himself

Ainsi, quand Harry Hapless pensait[35] qu'il était[36] au cinquième étage, il était en réalité au quatrième étage.

---

125 **5** Finalement, les vacances de Harry Hapless finissent. **La veille** de son départ il téléphone à la compagnie aérienne pour confirmer l'heure de son vol[37]. L'employée lui rappelle[38] que son avion est à 8 h 15.

130 Elle lui recommande d'être à l'aéroport une heure et demie avant le départ.

Le lendemain, Harry veut profiter[39] de son dernier jour en France. Le matin, il fait une promenade à pied et prend quelques photos.

135 À midi, il déjeune dans un bon restaurant. L'après-midi, il va dans les magasins et achète quelques souvenirs. Puis il retourne à son hôtel, paie sa **note** et prend un taxi. Arrivé à l'aéroport, il

140 regarde sa montre et dit: «Il est 6 heures 15. J'ai encore deux heures avant le départ de mon avion.» Puis il va au comptoir[40] de la compagnie aérienne. Là, l'hôtesse lui dit: «Mais, Monsieur Hapless, le dernier avion

145 pour New York est parti il y a dix minutes.»

---

[35] thought [36] was
[37] flight [38] reminds
[39] to take advantage [40] counter

MOTS CLÉS
la veille   the day before   **la note**   the bill

Qu'est-ce qui s'est passé[41]?

- En France, les avions sont souvent en avance.

150 - L'employée a donné à Harry un mauvais renseignement.

- Harry ne sait pas comment fonctionne l'heure officielle.

Interprétation

Harry ne sait pas comment fonctionne l'heure officielle.

155 En France, on utilise l'heure officielle pour donner l'heure des trains, des avions, etc. L'heure officielle commence à 0 heure le matin et finit à 23 heures 59 le soir.

Harry Hapless pensait que son avion
160 était à 8 h 15 du soir (ou 20 h 15 à l'heure officielle). En réalité, l'avion était à 8 h 15 du matin.

---

[41] what happened?

Vocabulaire de la lecture

Mots clés

la vie quotidienne *daily life*
une habitude *a custom, habit*
le lendemain *the next day*
un jour férié *a holiday*
lent *slow*

énorme *large, enormous*
la veille *the day before*
la note *the bill*
le deuil *mourning*

A. Écrivez le mot clé dont le sens *(whose meaning)* est le plus proche *(closest)* du contraire *(opposite)* du mot donné.

1. rapide _____

2. petit _____

3. une nouveauté _____

4. un jour de travail _____

5. la joie _____

B. Faites un paragraphe pour décrire une semaine typique, en utilisant au moins trois des mots clés.

_____

_____

_____

_____

_____

_____

Tu as compris?

1. Pourquoi est-ce qu'Harry va à la banque?

_____

2. Comment est le service quand Harry va au restaurant?

_____

3. Qu'est-ce qu'Harry apporte chez son ami Jacques Lachance?

_____

4. Quand Harry va chez le dentiste, qui est-ce qu'il rencontre?

_____

5. Quand est-ce qu'Harry est arrivé à l'aéroport? Quand est-ce que son avion est parti?

_____

Connexion personnelle

Write a short letter to a French pen pal who is planning to come and visit you. In your letter, explain one or two things that your French friend might find different than in France.

Cher/Chère ami(e), C'est bientôt la date de ton arrivée.

Je t'écris pour expliquer les quelques choses qui sont

différentes aux États-Unis par rapport à la France.

Chez nous...

_____

_____

_____

_____

_____

_____

Avant de lire *Le véritoscope*

Reading Strategy

MAKE PREDICTIONS Read the title and subtitles and predict what this reading is about. After reading, decide whether you need to revise your prediction.

Your prediction _____

_____

_____

_____

How close was your prediction? _____

_____

What You Need To Know

In the reading, Monsieur Dumas is described as a **bricoleur de génie.** The French word **bricoleur** *(do-it-yourselfer),* is someone who engages in **bricolage.** Both words come from the verb **bricoler,** which means *to tinker* or *to fiddle.* The French have a long history of being excellent **bricoleurs,** and there are many stores in France that cater to them. The BHV, a large department store on the right bank in Paris, has an entire floor devoted to products for do-it-yourselfers, gives workshops on **bricolage,** and even has a café called the Café Atelier, whose motto is "Parlons bricolage!".

Bricolage can also have a negative connotation, though, as in our English term "jury-rigged".

Le véritoscope

1 Une mauvaise nouvelle

Ce matin, Monsieur Dumas, avocat, est arrivé tard[1] à son bureau. Quand il est entré, Julien, le comptable, l'attendait[2].

— Monsieur, je voudrais vous parler en privé[3].

5 — Mais qu'est-ce qu'il y a[4], Julien?

— Eh bien, monsieur, c'est arrivé encore une fois[5].

— Quoi?

— Quelqu'un a pris de l'argent dans la caisse.

10 — Combien?

— Cinq cents euros.

— Vous êtes sûr?

— Absolument sûr. J'ai compté[6] l'argent hier soir et je l'ai recompté ce matin. Il manque[7]

15 cinq cents euros.

— Bien, bien, merci! Je vais voir ce que je peux faire.

---

[1] late [2] was waiting for him [3] in private
[4] what's wrong [5] once again [6] counted
[7] … is missing

À réfléchir…

Explain the title. What do you think a **véritoscope** might be? **(Make inferences)**

READER'S SUCCESS STRATEGY You have probably noticed that in French, as in English, new words can be formed by adding prefixes. Here are some common French prefixes:

re- (meaning *again, back, away, over*)

in- (meaning *not* and corresponding to the English *in-, un-, dis-*)

mal- (meaning *evil* and corresponding to English *un-, dis-*)

sous- (meaning *under* and corresponding to the English *sub-*)

Find at least one example of a word with each prefix in the reading and circle it. Write the words and their meanings here.

Word	Meaning

2 Monsieur Dumas, en train de bricoler

Seul dans son bureau, Monsieur Dumas a **réfléchi** à la situation. C'est la troisième fois

20 en deux mois que «quelqu'un» **s'est servi** dans la caisse. La première fois, c'était[8] cent euros. La deuxième fois, c'était deux cents euros. Et maintenant, c'est cinq cents euros.

«Si cela continue comme cela[9], je vais bientôt[10]

25 être ruiné» a pensé Monsieur Dumas. «Oui, mais que faire? Appeler[11] la police? C'est inutile. La police a d'autres choses à faire. **Renvoyer** tous mes employés? C'est impossible. Un seul[12] est **coupable**… Ah, j'ai

30 trouvé la solution… »

Le week-end suivant. Monsieur Dumas n'est pas sorti comme d'habitude. Il n'a pas dîné en ville. Il n'est pas allé au théâtre. Il n'a pas joué au bridge à son club… Il est resté chez lui. Et

35 qu'est-ce qu'il a fait chez lui? Il est descendu dans son atelier. Il a travaillé jour et nuit sur un «projet spécial». Il faut dire[13] que Monsieur Dumas n'est pas seulement un brillant avocat. C'est aussi un bricoleur de génie[14].

---

[8] it was   [9] like that   [10] soon
[11] Call   [12] Only one person   [13] It should be said
[14] brilliant tinkerer

MOTS CLÉS
seul(e) alone
réfléchir to think, reflect
se servir to help oneself

renvoyer to fire (an employee)
coupable guilty

Discovering French, Nouveau! **Level 2**

3 La réunion de lundi matin

40 Lundi, Monsieur Dumas est sorti de chez lui avec un mystérieux paquet[15] sous le bras. Puis il est allé à son bureau. Là, il a convoqué[16] tous ses employés pour une réunion[17].

À dix heures, tout le monde était assis[18] autour
45 de[19] la grande table dans la salle de réunion[20]. Il y avait[21] Alice et Claudine, les deux assistantes de Monsieur Dumas, Julien, le comptable, Madeleine, la réceptionniste, Gilbert, le secrétaire, et Pierrot, le garçon de courses[22].

50 Monsieur Dumas est entré dans la salle avec son mystérieux paquet. Il a posé le paquet au centre de la table. Puis il a pris la parole[23].

— J'ai le regret de vous annoncer qu'il y a un voleur[24] parmi[25] vous.

55 Silence dans la salle.

Monsieur Dumas a continué.

— À trois reprises[26] différentes, quelqu'un a pris de l'argent dans la caisse. Si le coupable **se dénonce,** je lui demanderai[27] de restituer[28]
60 l'argent et l'affaire sera réglée[29]. Est-ce que le coupable veut se dénoncer?

Personne n'a répondu.

— Eh bien, puisque[30] personne n'est coupable, vous ne verrez pas[31] d' inconvénient à vous
65 soumettre au test de vérité.

---

[15] package	[16] called together	[17] meeting	[18] seated
[19] around	[20] conference room	[21] There were	[22] errand boy
[23] began to speak	[24] thief	[25] among	[26] occasions
[27] will ask	[28] to return	[29] the matter will be settled	
[30] since	[31] won't see		

MOTS CLÉS
se dénoncer to give oneself up

Monsieur Dumas a ouvert[32] le mystérieux paquet. Les employés ont vu une étrange machine. L'élément central était un petit récipient rempli[33] d'eau. À ce récipient étaient

70 attachés des électrodes, des fils[34] électriques et un compteur.

— Cette machine s'appelle un véritoscope. C'est une machine ultrasensible qui capte[35] les impulsions nerveuses de l'individu[36]. Son

75 fonctionnement est très simple. Elle est reliée[37] à une lampe dans mon bureau. Vous mettez la main dans l'eau et vous dites une phrase. Si vous dites la vérité, rien ne se passe[38]. Si vous ne dites pas la vérité, la machine détecte

80 votre nervosité et la lampe qui est dans mon bureau **s'allume.** Évidemment,[39] cette machine fonctionne seulement[40] dans l'obscurité[41] la plus complète.

— Qu'est-ce qu'on fait? a demandé

85 Madeleine, la réceptionniste.

— Et bien, vous allez tour à tour[42] mettre la main dans l'eau et vous allez dire: «Ce n'est pas moi qui ai pris l'argent.»

— Mais puisque personne n'est coupable… ,

90 a dit Pierrot, le garçon de courses.

— Alors, vous n'avez rien à craindre[43]. C'est simplement un test pour confirmer votre innocence.

[32] opened	[33] filled (with)	[34] wires
[35] picks up	[36] person	[37] linked
[38] nothing happens	[39] Obviously	[40] only
[41] darkness	[42] one after the other	[43] nothing to fear

MOTS CLÉS
s'allumer to light up

4 Le moment de vérité

Monsieur Dumas a éteint[44] les **lumières** et il
95 est sorti. Il est allé à son bureau où il a attendu
dix minutes. Puis il est retourné dans la salle
de réunion.

— Alors, est-ce que la lampe s'est allumée? a
demandé Alice, la première assistante.

100 — Non, elle ne s'est pas allumée, a répondu
Monsieur Dumas.

— Vous voyez, personne ici n'est malhonnête,
a ajouté Claudine, la seconde assistante.

— Est-ce qu'on peut sortir? a demandé
105 Gilbert, le secrétaire.

— Attendez un peu, a dit Monsieur Dumas.
Montrez-moi d'abord vos mains.

Tout le monde a levé les mains.

— Eh bien, maintenant, je sais qui est le
110 coupable. Voilà, j'ai oublié de vous dire que
dans le liquide il y a un produit[45] **incolore** qui
devient vert au contact de **la peau.**

— C'est vrai, j'ai la main verte, a dit
Madeleine.

115 — Et moi aussi, a dit Pierrot.

— Mais vous, Julien, a dit Monsieur Dumas,
vous avez la main blanche. Expliquez-nous
donc pourquoi vous n'avez pas voulu vous
soumettre au test du véritoscope!

---

[44] turned off   [45] (chemical) product

CHALLENGE Why do you think
Julien told Monsieur Dumas
about the missing money?
(Draw Conclusions)

À réfléchir...

Why didn't Julien put his
hands in the water? **(Draw
conclusions)**

MOTS CLÉS
une lumière light
incolore colorless

la peau skin

Vocabulaire de la lecture

Mots clés

seul(e) *alone*

réfléchir *to think, reflect*

se servir *to help oneself*

renvoyer *to fire (an employee)*

coupable *guilty*

se dénoncer *to give oneself up*

s'allumer *to light up*

une lumière *light*

incolore *colorless*

la peau *skin*

A. Écrivez le mot clé dont le sens est le plus proche du contraire du mot donné.

1. coloré _____

2. innocent _____

3. s'éteindre _____

4. engager _____

5. ensemble _____

B. Complétez chaque phrase par le mot clé qui convient le mieux.

1. Si je fais quelque chose de mauvais et je l'admets,

   je me _____.

2. Henri s'est coupé avec un couteau. Il va mettre un pansement *(bandage)*

   sur sa _____.

3. Il fait trop noir ici. Je vais mettre de la _____.

4. C'est difficile de savoir ce que je dois faire.

   Laisse-moi _____ un peu.

5. Dans la chambre d'hôtel, on peut _____ des objets dans la
   salle de bains.

Tu as compris?

1. Quel est le problème de Monsieur Dumas?

_____

2. Pourquoi est-ce que Monsieur Dumas ne peut pas renvoyer tous ses employés?

_____

3. Comment a-t-il passé son week-end?

_____

4. Qu'est-ce que Monsieur Dumas annonce à ses employés à la réunion de lundi matin?

_____

5. Comment Monsieur Dumas sait-il que c'est Julien le coupable?

_____

Connexion personnelle

Bricolage can cover a wide variety of do-it-yourself projects. What types of things do you like to do around the house? Make a list on the notebook page.

Projets à la maison

Avant de lire   *La maison hantée*

Reading Strategy

SKIM FOR THE GIST Be sure to look over titles, subtitles, and any images to get an overall idea of the reading. Look at the drawing of the house to familiarize yourself with new vocabulary before you start to read.

SCAN FOR SPECIFIC INFORMATION Scan for the following information.

1. le nom du village où Jean-François habitait quand il avait quatorze ans _____

2. le nom de son camarade de classe _____

3. une expression qui veut dire «chicken» en français _____

What You Need To Know

Marcillac is a small village located in the Limousin region of France. With approximately 1,000 inhabitants, Marcillac is intimate in size but still supports a thriving tourist industry with its lake, two beaches and campgrounds. Of the many trees that make up the forests around Marcillac, the chestnut tree is one of the most useful, supplying both wood and chestnuts, which play a large role in local cuisine. Located in the Massif Central, Limousin is perhaps best known for its regional capital, Limoges, the city made famous by enamels and porcelains.

Une vieille maison hantée

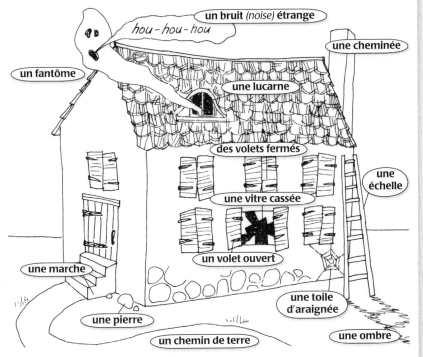

- un bruit (noise) étrange
- hou-hou-hou
- un fantôme
- une cheminée
- une lucarne
- des volets fermés
- une échelle
- une vitre cassée
- un volet ouvert
- une marche
- une toile d'araignée
- une pierre
- un chemin de terre
- une ombre

À réfléchir...

Number the following events in the correct order. (**Sequence of Events**)

_____ Il commence à pleuvoir.

_____ Jean-François monte dans le grenier.

_____ Une chouette effrayé s'envole.

_____ Benoit et Jean-François entendent *hou-hou-hou*.

_____ Benoît invite Jean-François à visiter la maison hantée avec lui.

A Le défi

Je m'appelle Jean-François Dupré. J'ai 21 ans et je suis étudiant. J'habite à Paris, mais en réalité je ne suis pas parisien. Ma famille est originaire de province[1].

5 Quand j' avais 14 ans, ma famille s'est installée[2] à Marcillac, une petite ville dans le centre de la France. La raison de ce déplacement[3] est que mon père venait d'être nommé sous-directeur de la banque locale.

10 Nous avons vécu deux ans là-bas.

---

[1] comes from one of the French provinces   [2] settled   [3] move

À MARQUER ⟩ GRAMMAIRE

In this unit, you've learned how to use both the **imparfait** and the **passé composé** in relating past stories. In the boxed section of the text, underline verbs in the **passé composé** and circle verbs in the **imparfait**. Notice how each is used.

Comme[4] nous étions nouveaux au village,
je n' avais pas beaucoup d'amis. J' avais un
camarade de classe qui s'appelait Benoît.
Nous étions voisins, mais nous n' étions pas
15 vraiment copains. Nous allions ensemble[5] à
l'école, et parfois nous jouions au foot après
les classes, mais c' était tout.

Benoît avait 14 ans comme moi, mais il était
plus grand et beaucoup plus fort que moi. Ce
20 qui m'irritait en lui, c'est qu'il voulait toujours
avoir raison et quand nous jouions à un jeu, il
voulait toujours gagner.

Un jour, pendant les vacances de printemps,
Benoît m'a demandé: «Dis, Jean-François, est-
25 ce que tu veux aller explorer la maison hantée
avec moi?» La maison hantée, c'était une
vieille ferme abandonnée à deux kilomètres
du village. J'avais bien envie d'aller visiter la
maison hantée, mais je ne voulais pas y aller
30 avec Benoît. Je lui ai répondu…

— Non, merci! Je ne me sens pas très bien
aujourd'hui.

— Tu ne te sens pas très bien? Ah, oh,… dis
plutôt[6] que tu te dégonfles[7]…

35 — Non, je ne me dégonfle pas.

— Si, tu te dégonfles parce que tu as peur des
fantômes… Ha, ha, ha!

---

[4] since   [5] together   [6] rather
[7] you are losing courage (lit. becoming deflated)

READING TIP Dialogue in French is often marked by the use of dashes.

— Je n'ai pas peur des fantômes plus que toi.

— Alors, dans ce cas[8], viens avec moi. Si tu ne
40   viens pas, je vais dire à tout le monde que tu
es une poule mouillée[9].

B L'expedition

J'ai bien été obligé d'accepter **le
défi** de Benoît. Je suis allé chez moi
prendre une lampe de poche[10] et je suis parti
45   avec Benoît… sans rien dire à mes parents.

Nous sommes sortis du village et nous
sommes allés dans la direction de la maison
hantée. Nous avons d'abord pris un chemin
de terre, puis nous avons marché à travers
50   champs[11]. Finalement, nous sommes arrivés
devant la ferme. J'ai regardé ma montre. Il
était six heures et demie. La nuit commençait
à tomber.

La ferme était une grande maison
55   rectangulaire de deux étages avec un grenier.
Dans le village, on disait qu'elle était habitée
par le fantôme d'un ancien[12] fermier, assassiné
par des brigands[13] au siècle dernier[14]. C'est vrai
que, isolée au milieu des[15] champs, la ferme
60   avait un aspect sinistre…

J'ai pris une pierre que j'ai lancée[16] dans la
porte et j'ai crié:

— Fantôme, es-tu là?

---

[8] in that case   [9] "chicken" (lit. wet hen)   [10] flashlight
[11] across the fields   [12] former   [13] robbers
[14] in the last century, 100 years ago   [15] in the middle of
[16] threw

MOTS CLÉS
un défi a challenge

— Arrête, a dit Benoît, on ne sait jamais…

65 — On ne sait jamais quoi? lui ai-je répondu.

— Euh, rien!

— Alors, on entre?

— Écoute, Jean-François, on peut peut-être revenir demain. Regarde, il pleut.

70 C'est vrai, la pluie commençait à tomber. À vrai dire, j'avais aussi un peu peur, mais je voulais donner une leçon à Benoît. Alors, je lui ai dit:

— Dis donc, Benoît, tu ne veux pas entrer 75 dans la maison, hein? C'est toi la poule mouillée!

— Non, mais dis donc, ça ne va pas[17]?

 Dans la maison hantée

Nous avons donc décidé d'entrer dans la maison. Oui, mais comment?

80 La porte était fermée. Les volets aussi étaient fermés à l'exception d'un volet du salon. Nous avons cassé une vitre et nous sommes entrés par la fenêtre. À l'intérieur, il faisait très noir. J'ai allumé ma lampe de poche et nous avons 85 exploré les pièces du rez-de-chaussée.

La maison était vraiment abandonnée. Le salon, la salle à manger, la cuisine, tout était vide[18]… Maintenant, on entendait la pluie qui tombait de plus en plus fort[19]. C'était sinistre.

---

[17] are you crazy?   [18] empty   [19] harder and harder

90 J'ai dit à Benoît: «Tu me suis[20]? Nous allons explorer le premier étage.» Je n'avais vraiment pas envie d'aller au premier étage, mais je voulais voir ce que Benoît allait faire.

«D'accord, je te suis, mais ne va pas trop vite», 95 a-t-il répondu. Nous avons monté l'escalier en faisant très attention[21] car[22] les marches n'étaient pas très solides. Le premier étage était encore plus désolé et plus sinistre que le rez-de-chaussée. Des piles de vieux journaux 100 traînaient[23] sur le sol. Les murs étaient couverts de toiles d'araignées. Dans la salle de bains, le lavabo et la baignoire étaient cassés.

Tout à coup, l'orage s'est mis à[24] éclater. Un coup de tonnerre, suivi d'un autre coup de 105 tonnerre… Puis, entre les coups de tonnerre, un bruit beaucoup plus étrange.

Hou, hou, hou, hou, hou…

— Tu as entendu? m'a demandé Benoît.
— Oui, j'ai entendu.

110 *Hou, hou, hou…*

Le bruit étrange venait du grenier.

Hou, hou, hou…

J'ai dit à Benoît:

—Je vais voir ce que c'est.

115 — Non, non, c'est le fantôme. Ne monte pas. Reste avec moi. J'ai peur…, a supplié[25] Benoît.
— Écoute, reste ici si tu veux, mais moi, je vais dans le grenier.

---

[20] Are you following me?   [21] being very careful   [22] because
[23] were lying around   [24] began to   [25] begged

CHALLENGE What is your opinion of Benoît? (Make Judgments)

Le fantôme

Moi aussi, j'avais terriblement peur, mais je ne pouvais plus **reculer.**

120 Alors, je suis allé jusqu'à l'échelle qui menait[26] au grenier.

Hou, hou, hou…

Je ne sais pas comment j'ai eu la force de monter à l'échelle, mais bientôt[27] j'étais dans le
125 grenier. J'ai alors vu le «fantôme». C'était **une chouette effrayée** par l'intrusion de visiteurs dans son domaine. Alors, j'ai ouvert une lucarne[28] et la chouette **s'est envolée** dans la nature… J'ai regardé **dehors.** J'ai vu aussi une
130 ombre qui courait. C'était Benoît.

Je lui ai crié: «Hé, Benoît! N'aie pas peur! J'ai découvert le fantôme… C'est une vieille chouette. Attends-moi!»

Mais Benoît ne m'a pas entendu. Et il a
135 continué à courir à toute vitesse dans la direction du village.

---

[26] led   [27] soon   [28] skylight

MOTS CLÉS

reculer to back up, back down	**s'envoler** to fly off
une chouette an owl	**dehors** outside
effrayer to frighten	

Vocabulaire de la lecture

Mots clés

un défi *a challenge*

reculer *to back up, back down*

une chouette *an owl*

effrayer *to frighten*

s'envoler *to fly off*

dehors *outside*

un grenier *attic*

la baignoire *bathtub*

les murs *walls*

le sol *floor*

A. Décidez si les deux mots constituent des antonymes ou des synonymes.

	ANTONYME	SYNONYME
1. avancer – reculer	_____	_____
2. effrayer – faire peur	_____	_____
3. s'envoler – atterrir *(to land)*	_____	_____
4. dehors – dedans	_____	_____

B. Complétez chaque phrase par le mot clé qui convient le mieux.

1. Benoît a posé un _____ à Jean-François.

2. Quand les garçons ont visité la maison hantée, il y avait

une _____ qui faisait *hou hou hou.*

3. Souvent, on met des vieilles choses qu'on voudrait garder

dans le _____.

4. On prend un bain dans la _____.

5. On met des posters sur les _____.

Tu as compris?

1. Pourquoi est-ce que Jean-François n'aimait pas Benoît?

_____

2. Quel est le défi de Benoît?

_____

3. Pourquoi est-ce que Jean-François a insisté pour visiter la maison même après que la pluie tombait?

_____

4. Pourquoi Benoît ne voulait-il pas monter au grenier?

_____

5. Qu'est-ce qui était à l'origine du bruit mystérieux?

_____

Connexion personnelle

Are there any "haunted houses" in your neighborhood? Use the notebook page to write a short paragraph describing a house or abandoned piece of property near you.

Une maison hantée

Avant de lire   *L'affaire des bijoux*

Reading Strategy

SKIM Before reading a long passage, it is helpful to read quickly to get a general idea of its content. Skim the paragraphs, noting clues that indicate the central theme or topic. Then, do a more careful reading. After skimming *L'affaire des bijoux,* write down some words or phrases that indicate what it is about.

_____

_____

_____

_____

MAKE PREDICTIONS Remember that an active reader makes predictions as he or she reads. See if you can figure out who is responsible for the crime in the story.

What You Need To Know

France has long been known as a producer of luxury goods, including jewelry. In Paris, the place to buy expensive jewelry is the Place Vendôme. Originally designed by the same architect who designed Versailles, the Place Vendôme was planned by Louis XIV to be a square of public buildings, with his statue in the center. Attacked during the French Revolution as a symbol of the monarchy, the Place Vendôme was redesigned by Napoleon I, who modified its shape and had a column erected in the center of the Place, topped with a statue of himself dressed as a Roman. Today, the Place Vendôme is occupied by luxury offices and shops, as well as hotels.

READING TIP This reading is divided into five sections and an epilogue. After you read each section, take a minute to write down the main idea of each section. Give each section a possible title.

L'affaire des bijoux

Chatel-Royan, 28 juillet

La série des vols de bijoux continue

Pour la troisième fois en un mois, un bijoutier[1] de notre ville a été victime d'un audacieux **malfaiteur.** M. Kramer, propriétaire de la **bijouterie** Au Bijou d'Or, a signalé à la police la disparition de plusieurs diamants de grande valeur[2]. Comme[3] les fois précédentes, le **vol** a été découvert peu après le passage dans la bijouterie d'un mystérieux monsieur blond. Selon la description donnée par M. Kramer, l'homme portait des lunettes de soleil et un imperméable beige. Il parlait avec un léger accent britannique. La police continue son enquête[4].

5

10

15 **Q**uelques jours plus tard...

Monsieur Rochet, propriétaire de la bijouterie Top Bijou, a engagé une nouvelle employée. Bien entendu[5], il lui a recommandé d'être très prudente:

[1] jeweler   [2] value   [3] like   [4] investigation   [5] Of course

MOTS CLÉS
bijoux jewels, jewelry
un malfaiteur a criminal

une bijouterie a jewelry store
un vol a theft

20 — Soyez très vigilante, mademoiselle! Vous savez que des vols importants ont été commis[6] dans les bijouteries de notre ville. Je ne veux pas être la prochaine victime.

— Vous pouvez compter sur moi, Monsieur
25 Rochet! Je vais faire très attention.

Ce matin-là, il n'y a pas beaucoup de clients à Top Bijou. La première cliente est une vieille dame. Elle demande à regarder des médailles. Peu après, un autre client entre
30 dans la boutique. Il est blond et très élégant. Il ne porte pas de lunettes de soleil, mais il a un imperméable beige sur le bras.

Monsieur Rochet appelle son employée:

— C'est certainement lui. Faites très, très
35 attention, mais ne soyez pas trop nerveuse. Je suis là. Si quelque chose arrive, je déclenche[7] le signal d'alarme.

L'employée accueille[8] le client.

— Bonjour, monsieur. Vous désirez?
40 — Je voudrais une bague…

L'employée remarque que l'homme parle avec un accent étranger[9]. Elle tourne nerveusement les yeux vers[10] Monsieur Rochet. Celui-ci[11] reste très calme.

45 L'employée est rassurée.

— C'est pour un homme ou pour une femme?

— Pour une femme.

---

[6] commited   [7] set off   [8] welcomes
[9] foreign   [10] toward   [11] the latter

À MARQUER ▷ GRAMMAIRE

You've learned how to make comparisons with adjectives—to say something is more expensive or less expensive, for example. Reread the boxed section of the text and find two examples of comparisons with adjectives.

À réfléchir...

Why does Monsieur Rochet's new employee become nervous when the customer asks to see the most expensive jewelry? **(Draw Conclusions)**

READER'S SUCCESS STRATEGY   There is a lot of text in this reading. Use a ruler to help you read slowly and deliberately. Place the ruler under the first line of text. When you finish reading the line, move the ruler down to the next line.

Prudemment, l'employée montre quelques bagues assez bon marché au client. Celui-ci
50 répond:

— Ces bagues sont jolies, mais vous avez certainement mieux.

> L'employée montre d'autres bagues beaucoup plus chères au client qui ne semble pas
> 55 satisfait.
>
> — Ces bagues sont plus jolies, mais je cherche quelque chose de vraiment exceptionnel. C'est pour l'anniversaire de ma femme.

L'employée jette un coup d'oeil désespéré[12]
60 vers Monsieur Rochet. Celui-ci, impassible, lui dit:

— Eh bien, mademoiselle, qu'est-ce que vous attendez? Montrez à monsieur la «collection Top Bijou».

65 L'employée va chercher dans une vitrine[13] un plateau[14] de bagues ornées d'émeraudes[15], de rubis et de diamants de plusieurs carats. C'est la «collection Top Bijou».

Le client examine chaque bague sous la
70 surveillance de Monsieur Rochet et de son employée. Finalement, il choisit une bague ornée d'un gros rubis.

— Voilà, c'est cette bague que je voudrais acheter. Combien coûte-t-elle?

75 — Cent mille euros.

---

[12] glances desperately [13] store window
[14] tray [15] ring set with emeralds

— Cent mille euros? Très bien. Est-ce que je peux payer par chèque?

Monsieur Rochet est très prudent.

— Excusez-nous, monsieur, mais la maison
80 accepte seulement les traveller's chèques. Pouvez-vous payer en travellers?

— Oui, monsieur. C'était mon intention.

— Très bien. Est-ce que vous voulez un paquet-cadeau[16]?

85 — Oui, s'il vous plaît.

— Mademoiselle, est-ce que vous pouvez faire un paquet-cadeau pour monsieur?

L'employée va dans l'arrière-boutique[17] préparer le paquet. Pendant ce temps, le client signe les
90 traveller's chèques sous le regard extrêmement vigilant de Monsieur Rochet. L'employée revient dans la boutique avec un joli paquet.

— Voici votre paquet, monsieur.

— Merci, mademoiselle… Au revoir,
95 mademoiselle.

— Au revoir, monsieur.

Le client sort de la boutique.

L'employée s'adresse alors à la première cliente. Mais celle-ci sort de la boutique sans
100 acheter de médaille.

Après le départ de la vieille dame, l'employée va trouver Monsieur Rochet.

— Eh bien, dites donc[18], j'ai eu peur.

— À vrai dire[19], moi aussi!

---

[16] gift-wrapped   [17] back of the store
[18] hey! I say   [19] to tell the truth

105 — J'ai vraiment pensé que c'était lui le
malfaiteur.

— Et même si c'est lui, cela n'a pas
d'importance[20]. Il m'a payé! Regardez… cent
mille euros en traveller's chèques.

110 Quelques minutes plus tard…

L'employée va remettre la «collection Top
Bijou» dans la vitrine. Elle a alors une surprise
très désagréable.

— Monsieur Rochet, Monsieur Rochet!

115 — Qu'est-ce qu'il y a?

— Venez voir, les diamants ont disparu[21]!

— Mon Dieu, ce n'est pas possible!

Monsieur Rochet est bien obligé de se rendre à
l'évidence[22]. Il manque trois bagues serties[23] de
120 gros diamants. Les trois bagues les plus chères
de la boutique… Trois bagues qui valent[24] plus
de trois cent mille euros chacune!

— J'appelle la police tout de suite!

Grâce à[25] la signature sur les chèques et à
125 la description donnée par Monsieur Rochet
et son employée, la police n'a eu aucune[26]
difficulté à arrêter le client de la bijouterie.

---

[20] that doesn't matter   [21] disappeared   [22] face facts
[23] set   [24] are worth   [25] thanks to
[26] … not any, no

Le lendemain[27], l'article suivant a paru dans *L'Écho du Centre*:

Chatel-Royan, 6 août
Le voleur de bijoux arrêté

130 La police a arrêté hier soir un certain Sven Ericsen, touriste suédois, de passage dans notre ville. M. 135 Rochet, propriétaire de la bijouterie Top Bijou, et son employée, Mlle Picard, ont formellement identifié 140 ce personnage comme étant[28] l'auteur d'un vol de trois bagues. M. Ericsen a reconnu avoir rendu visite à la bijouterie, mais il nie[29] catégoriquement le vol. Malgré[30] une longue perquisition[31] dans la chambre de M. Ericsen à l'Hôtel Excelsior, la police n'a pas encore retrouvé la trace des bijoux, à l'exception d'une bague que le touriste suédois affirme avoir payée en traveller's chèques.

Pour la dixième fois, une vieille dame relit 145 l'article publié dans *L'Écho du Centre*. Cette vieille dame est la première cliente de la bijouterie. Elle pense: «La police n'a pas retrouvé les bijoux? Tiens, c'est curieux! Moi, je sais où ils sont. Mais d'abord, je dois vérifier 150 quelque chose.» Elle se lève et va téléphoner.

---

[27] the next day   [28] as (being)   [29] denies
[30] despite   [31] search

— Ah bon? Tu es absolument sûr? Alors, dans ce cas, je vais à la police immédiatement.

La vieille dame met son chapeau, prend sa canne et sort.

155 Une demi-heure plus tard, elle se trouve[32] dans le bureau de l'inspecteur.

— Alors, Inspecteur, est-ce que vous avez retrouvé les bijoux?

— Non, non, pas encore! Mais nous avons 160 arrêté le voleur. Il n'a pas encore confessé son crime, mais ce n'est qu'une affaire de temps[33]!

— Ce n'est pas parce que vous avez arrêté quelqu'un que cette personne est coupable[34].

— Qu'est-ce que vous dites? Le voleur a été 165 formellement identifié par Monsieur Rochet et son employée.

— Je dis que vous faites erreur[35].

— Mais c'est impossible!

— Moi aussi, j'étais dans la bijouterie au 170 moment de la disparition des bijoux. J'ai tout vu et je sais où sont les trois bagues de diamants.

— Mais…

— Suivez-moi[36], Inspecteur.

175 — Mais, où allons-nous?

— À la bijouterie, pour la reconstitution du vol! Et n'oubliez pas de prendre votre passe-partout[37]!

---

[32] is
[33] it's only a matter of time
[34] guilty
[35] are making a mistake
[36] Follow me
[37] passkey

L'inspecteur Poiret et la vieille dame entrent
180 dans la bijouterie. Monsieur Rochet est seul à
l'intérieur.

— Bonjour, Inspecteur! Alors, vous avez
retrouvé mes bijoux?

— Non, Monsieur Rochet. Mais madame
185 prétend[38] savoir où ils sont.

— Eh bien, où sont-ils?

La vieille dame prend la parole[39].

— Ils sont là… Dans ce tiroir[40]!

Monsieur Rochet devient très pâle.

190 — Mais c'est impossible, madame. Les bijoux
ont été volés. Le voleur a été arrêté!

L'inspecteur s'adresse au bijoutier:

— Ouvrez ce tiroir, s'il vous plaît.

Monsieur Rochet est devenu de plus en plus[41]
195 pâle.

— Euh, c'est que j'ai laissé la clé chez moi.

La vieille dame se tourne alors vers
l'inspecteur.

— Inspecteur, pouvez-vous ouvrir le tiroir?

200 L'inspecteur Poiret prend son passe-partout et
ouvre le tiroir. À l'intérieur, tout au fond[42], il y

---

[38] claims
[40] drawer
[42] all the way at the back

[39] speaks, takes the floor
[41] more and more

a trois magnifiques bagues. Monsieur Rochet
paraît[43] très surpris.

— Ça alors! Mais qui a pu mettre les bagues
205 dans ce tiroir? Vraiment, je ne comprends pas.
Je vais demander à mon employée si elle a
remarqué quelque chose.

La vieille dame lui répond:

— Allons, Monsieur Rochet, ne faites pas
210 l'innocent[44]. C'est vous-même[45] qui les avez
mises dans le tiroir.

— Moi?

— Oui, vous! J'étais là. Je vous ai vu. Quand
votre employée est allée dans l'arrière-
215 boutique, vous avez discrètement sorti les
bagues du plateau et vous les avez mises dans
votre poche[46]. Après le départ de votre client,
vous avez mis les bagues dans le tiroir et vous
l'avez fermé à clé.

220 — Mais, c'est ridicule! Pourquoi voler mes
propres[47] bagues?

— À cause de[48] l'assurance[49]! Hier après-
midi, après le constat[50] de la police, vous avez
téléphoné à votre compagnie d'assurance et
225 vous avez réclamé un million d'euros.

— Mais comment savez-vous cela?

— Ce matin, j'ai téléphoné à mon cousin.
C'est lui le directeur de votre compagnie
d'assurance. Il m'a tout expliqué.

230 — Qu'est-ce que vous inventez là?

[43] seems	[44] act innocent	[45] yourself	[46] pocket
[47] own	[48] because of	[49] insurance	[50] report

— Je n'invente rien. Vous êtes en difficultés financières.

Vous avez besoin d'argent. Alors, vous profitez de la série de vols qui affligent[51] les
235 bijoutiers de notre ville pour simuler un vol dans votre propre boutique.

Hier matin, vous avez vu entrer un client ressemblant vaguement au signalement de la police. C'était l'occasion idéale pour
240 commettre votre crime!

— Cette femme est folle!

L'inspecteur intervient.

— C'est inutile, Monsieur Rochet. Suivez-moi au poste de police.

Épilogue

245 Sven Ericsen est rentré chez lui avec les excuses de la police.

La vieille dame a reçu[52] une médaille de la compagnie d'assurance et les félicitations du maire[53] de Chatel-Royan.

250 L'inspecteur Poiret a reçu une promotion. Monsieur Rochet attend d'être jugé.

---

[51] afflict   [52] received   [53] mayor

CHALLENGE Were you suspicious of the blond customer in Monsieur Rochet's bijouterie? Why or why not? **(Make Judgments)**

Vocabulaire de la lecture

Mots clés

un vol   *a theft*

un malfaiteur   *a criminal*

une bijouterie   *a jewelry store*

les lunettes de soleil   *sunglasses*

un imperméable   *a raincoat*

une médaille   *a medal*

une bague   *a ring*

cher, chère   *expensive*

A. Mettez en regard le mot clé sur la gauche avec le mot ou l'expression qui l'explique.

_____ **1.** un malfaiteur

_____ **2.** les lunettes de soleil

_____ **3.** un imperméable

_____ **4.** une bague

a. un bijou qu'on donne à quelqu'un quand on se marie

b. quelqu'un qui fait de mauvaises choses (contre la loi)

c. on les porte sur les yeux

d. ce qu'on porte quand il pleut

B. Complétez chaque phrase par le mot clé qui convient le mieux.

1. Paul a acheté mon collier à cette _____.

2. Quand j'ai gagné la course, on m'a donné une _____.

3. Elle voulait acheter une nouvelle robe, mais elle était

trop _____.

4. Appelle la police! Il y a eu un _____ ici!

Tu as compris?

1. Quelle est la description du voleur, selon Monsieur Kramer?

_____

_____

2. Décrivez la visite du client à la bijouterie. Comment est-il? Qu'est-ce qu'il achète?

_____

_____

3. Quelle est la désagréable surprise de Mademoiselle Picard?

_____

4. Pourquoi est-ce que la vieille dame va voir l'inspecteur de police?

_____

5. Pourquoi Monsieur Rochet a-t-il simulé ce vol?

_____

Connexion personnelle

What kind of jewelry do you like? Use the notebook paper to design a piece of jewelry. Would it be a ring? Necklace? Watch? In gold or silver? With diamonds? Rubies? Write a few sentences about the kind of jewelry you like.

Mon bijou

Avant de lire   *La chasse au trésor*

Reading Strategy

PREDICT This is a different kind of story—a **chasse au trésor**—or treasure hunt. Many of the reading strategies you've learned might not be applicable here. For example, you don't want to jump ahead and skim the entire reading. This time, you want to wait and read each section separately. You can still preview the graphics to help give you a sense of what lies ahead. Look at the map. Skim section 0, Départ. Now, write down some predictions you have about the reading.

_____

_____

_____

_____

What You Need To Know

Have you ever read those "make-your-own-adventure" books? This reading is like that. Each step along the way will ask you to make a decision—and each decision will in turn decide your next step. Follow the directions you receive until you come to the end and discover the treasure. Don't cheat— read only those sections that apply to you. When you've finished, you can compare your route with your classmates.

LA CHASSE AU TRÉSOR

Veux-tu participer à une chasse au trésor?
C'est facile. Lis attentivement les instructions
suivantes.

Dans ce texte, tu vas faire une promenade
5   à vélo. Pendant cette promenade, tu devras
choisir certaines options. Tu auras aussi
l'occasion de découvrir certains objets cachés[1]
et de prendre certaines photos. Comment
découvriras - tu le trésor? Essaie de **rapporter**
10 le plus grand nombre d'objets et de photos.
(Marque toutes ces choses sur une liste comme
celle en bas de la page.) Mais attention, toutes
ces choses (objets ou photos) ne sont pas
équivalentes. Une seule te donnera l'accès au
15 trésor!

Es-tu prêt(e) maintenant? Va au (DÉPART) et
bonne chance!

Je m'arrête ...	De ma promenade, je ramène ...	
ÉTAPES	OBJETS	PHOTOS
10	•	• photo du lac
20		

---
[1] hidden

MOTS CLÉS
rapporter   to bring back

À réfléchir...

Of all the places you could
go on the bike route, which
ones would you most like to
visit and why? **(Analyze)**

À MARQUER > GRAMMAIRE
In this unit, you've been
learning to use the future
tense. In the opening section,
circle all the examples of the
future tense. Write them here,
along with their infinitives.

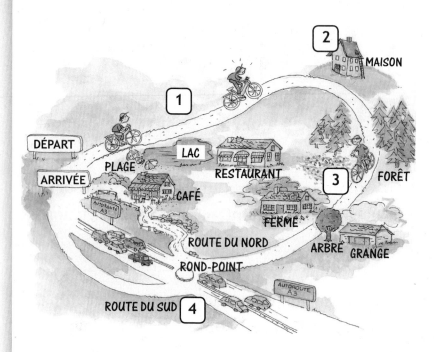

0 DÉPART

C'est samedi matin. Qu'est-ce que tu vas
faire aujourd'hui? Cela dépend du temps. Tu
écoutes la radio. La météo[2] annonce du beau
temps avec possibilité d'averses[3] dans l'après-
midi. Tu décides de faire une promenade à
vélo dans la campagne. Tu prends ton sac à
dos. Dans ton sac, tu mets ton imperméable,
ton maillot de bain, une lampe de poche,
une carte de la région et ton nouvel appareil-
photo. Tous ces objets te seront peut-être utiles
pendant ta promenade. Tu prends aussi une
bouteille de limonade et deux sandwichs.

---

[2] weather report   [3] showers

Va au 10

10 À MIDI

30 Il est midi. Tu as fait 20 kilomètres. Tu es un peu fatigué(e) et tu as faim. Tu t'arrêtes près d'un lac. Il y a une belle plage. Il y a aussi une pancarte[4] qui indique: Restaurant du Lac à 200 mètres.

35 **Qu'est-ce que tu feras?**

- Tu t'arrêteras cinq minutes. Tu mangeras tes sandwichs, puis tu continueras ta promenade. **Va au** ⎡10⎤

- Tu prendras une photo du lac et
40 après tu feras un pique-nique sur la plage. **Va au** ⎡11⎤

- Tu iras au Restaurant du Lac. **Va au** ⟨101⟩

~~~~~~~~~~

11 APRÈS LE PIQUE-NIQUE

Tu as mangé tes deux sandwichs et tu as bu de la limonade.

45 Tu es reposé(e) maintenant.

Qu'est-ce que tu feras après?

- Tu continueras ta promenade. **Va au** ⎡20⎤

- Tu iras nager. **Va au** ⎡12⎤

- Tu rentreras chez toi. **Va au** ⟨100⟩

[4] sign

READING TIP You've learned about cognates, but there are also **faux amis**—words that look alike in French and English but have *different* meanings. There are several **faux amis** in this reading. See if you can tell from context what each of them means. Write the meanings here.

une cave _____

un pot _____

un coin _____

une pièce _____

12 SUR LA PLAGE

50 Tu mets ton maillot de bain et tu vas nager. C'est un véritable plaisir de nager ici. L'eau est pure et pas très froide. Tu nages pendant dix minutes et tu sors de l'eau.

Qu'est-ce que tu feras après?

55 • Tu t'habilleras et tu continueras ta promenade à vélo. **Va au** 20

• Tu prendras une photo de la plage et tu feras une petite promenade à pied. **Va au** 13

13 LE PORTE-MONNAIE

Tu marches sur une belle plage de sable[5] fin.
60 Tout à coup[6] ton pied heurte quelque chose. Qu'est-ce que c'est? Tu cherches l'objet caché dans le sable. C'est un porte-monnaie[7].

Tu ouvres ce porte-monnaie. Il n'y a pas de nom, pas d'adresse. Il y a seulement trois
65 choses: un billet de 50 euros, un billet de loterie et une clé. Tu peux choisir seulement une chose.

Qu'est-ce que tu choisiras?

• le billet de 50 euros
70 • le billet de loterie
• la clé
• Tu mettras la chose que tu as choisie dans ton sac et tu continueras ta promenade. **Va au** 20

---

[5] sand   [6] suddenly   [7] wallet

20 LA MAISON ABANDONNÉE

75 Tu pédales, tu pédales... Maintenant, tu montes une côte[8]. Oh là là, c'est difficile. Au sommet de la côte, tu aperçois une belle maison de pierre.

Ça y est! Tu es maintenant au sommet. Tu
80 arrives devant la maison. Surprise, c'est une maison abandonnée! La porte principale est fermée à clé. Sur la porte, il y a un écriteau[9]: «Interdiction d'entrer». Cette maison est mystérieuse et fascinante. Tu as bien envie de
85 la visiter.

Qu'est-ce que tu feras?

- Tu prendras une photo de la maison et tu continueras ta promenade. **Va au 30**

- Tu prendras une photo de la maison et
90 ensuite tu exploreras la maison malgré[10] l'interdiction. **Va au 21**

~~~~~~~~~~~~~~

21 PAR QUELLE ENTRÉE?

D'accord, tu veux explorer la maison, mais comment entrer? Ce n'est pas si difficile. Tu fais le tour de[11] la maison et tu découvres trois
95 entrées possibles. À droite, il y a une échelle qui **mène** à un grenier. À gauche, il y a une petite trappe qui ouvre sur une cave. Derrière, il y a une fenêtre ouverte qui mène dans la cuisine.

---

[8] hill [9] notice [10] in spite of [11] go around

MOTS CLÉS
mener to lead

100 **Qu'est-ce que tu feras?**

- Tu monteras au grenier
  par l'échelle.   **Va au** ⬦102⬦

- Tu descendras dans la cave
  par la trappe.   **Va au** [22]

105 - Tu entreras dans la cuisine
  par la fenêtre.   **Va au** [25]

~~~~~~~~~

[22] DANS LA CAVE

Tu descends dans la cave. Il fait froid et
humide… Cette cave est vraiment très noire.
Heureusement tu as pris ta lampe de poche,
110 mais est-ce que les piles[12] sont bonnes?

Vroum! Euh, qu'est-ce que c'est que ce bruit?
C'est une chauve-souris[13]! Ploc! Qu'est-ce que
c'est que cet autre bruit? C'est une brique qui
vient de tomber.

115 **Est-ce que tu veux vraiment continuer
l'exploration de la cave?**

- Oui, tu continueras
  l'exploration de la cave.   **Va au** [23]

- Non, mais tu entreras dans la maison
120 par la fenêtre de la cuisine.   **Va au** [25]

- Non, vraiment, cette maison est trop
  dangereuse. Tu sortiras de la cave et tu
  continueras ta promenade à vélo. **Va au** [30]

[12] batteries   [13] bat

~~~~~~~~~

23 DANS LE TUNNEL

Tu continues l'exploration de la cave. (Tu
125 as de la chance. Ta lampe fonctionne bien!)
Maintenant tu es dans un tunnel.

Ploc! Une autre brique tombe. Vroum! Une
autre chauve-souris passe. Tu avances très
lentement. Tu arrives à une bifurcation[14]. Il y a
130 un passage à droite et un passage à gauche.

Qu'est-ce que tu feras?

- Tu iras à droite.   **Va au** (24)

- Tu iras à gauche.   **Va au** (104)

~~~~~~~~~

24 LE PASSAGE DE DROITE

Le passage de droite mène à un mur. Tu ne
135 peux pas continuer. Le passage est bloqué. Tu
es fatigué(e) et, **avoue**-le, tu as un peu peur!

Qu'est-ce que tu feras?

- Tu exploreras le passage
  de gauche.   **Va au** (104)

140 - Tu sortiras de la cave et tu continueras
  ta promenade à vélo.   **Va au** (30)

[14] fork (in the road)

~~~~~~~~~

MOTS CLÉS
avouer to admit

25 DANS LA CUISINE

Tu réussis à entrer dans la cuisine par la fenêtre. (C'est assez facile parce que tu es très athlétique.)

145 Cette cuisine n'est vraiment pas très hospitalière[15]. Les murs, autrefois blancs, sont maintenant gris. Il y a des toiles d'araignée[16] partout[17]. Au centre de la cuisine, il y a une vieille table de métal. Autour de la table, il

150 y a six chaises cassées.

À gauche, il y a un placard avec l'inscription: «Attention! Danger!»

À droite, il y a un buffet. En face de la fenêtre, il y a une porte fermée.

155 Tu peux faire seulement l'une des choses suivantes.

Qu'est-ce que tu feras?

- Tu ouvriras le placard.   **Va au** ⟨103⟩

- Tu ouvriras le buffet.   **Va au** ⟨26⟩

160 • Tu ouvriras la porte.   **Va au** ⟨27⟩

〜〜〜〜〜〜

26 LE BUFFET

Le buffet est un buffet ancien. Il y a trois tiroirs. Dans chaque tiroir, il y a un objet différent. Dans le premier tiroir, il y a un pot de confiture. Dans le second tiroir, il y a une

165 assiette avec un dessin[18] qui représente un

---

[15] welcoming   [16] spider web
[17] everywhere   [18] drawing, picture

homme à cheval et l'inscription: «Waterloo 1814». Cette assiette est cassée. Dans le troisième tiroir, il y a une enveloppe avec des vieilles photos représentant des gens habillés
170 à la mode de 1900. Tu peux prendre seulement un objet avec toi.

Quel objet choisiras-tu?

- le pot de confiture?

- l'assiette?

175 - l'enveloppe avec les photos?

- Prends l'objet que tu as choisi et continue ta promenade à vélo. **Va au** (30)

~~~~~~~~~

27 DANS LA SALLE À MANGER

Tu ouvres la porte. Tu entres dans une grande pièce. C'est probablement la salle à manger
180 de la maison. Cette pièce est complètement vide[19]. Il n'y a rien sauf[20] un portrait ancestral au mur. Ce portrait représente une belle jeune femme avec un grand chapeau. Tu prends une photo de ce portrait. Il y a deux autres portres,
185 mais elles sont fermées à clé.

Qu'est ce que tu feras?

- Tu quitteras la maison et tu continueras ta promenade à vélo. **Va au** (30)

- Tu descendras dans la cave par
190 la petite trappe. **Va au** (22)

---

[19] empty   [20] except

~~~~~~~~~

30 LA PLUIE

Maintenant tu descends la côte. La descente est beaucoup plus facile que la montée.

Le **paysage** est magnifique. La route traverse d'abord une forêt de sapins[21]. Ensuite, elle
195 traverse des prairies et des champs couverts de fleurs. Là-bas, au loin, on peut voir une rivière. Malheureusement, il y a maintenant de gros nuages[22] noirs dans le ciel[23]. Bientôt, la pluie commence à tomber. Tu mets ton
200 imperméable. La pluie devient plus forte. Il y a des éclairs[24] et du tonnerre[25]. Tu décides de t'arrêter. Oui, mais où trouver un abri[26]?

Heureusement, il y a plusieurs possibilités. Sur le bord de[27] la route, il y a un grand
205 arbre. Un peu plus loin, il y a une grange. Si tu continues par un petit chemin, il y a une ferme avec une grande cheminée.

Qu'est-ce que tu feras?

• Tu iras sous l'arbre.   Va au (105)

210 • Tu iras dans la grange.   Va au [31]

• Tu iras dans la ferme.   Va au ◇106◇

---

[21] pine trees   [22] clouds   [23] sky
[24] lightning   [25] thunder   [26] shelter
[27] on the side of

MOTS CLÉS
le paysage   landscape, scenery

Discovering French, Nouveau! **Level 2**

31 DANS LA GRANGE

La grange n'est pas fermée à clé. Tu entres.
Cette grange est en réalité un garage. À
l'intérieur, il y a une grosse Peugeot noire.

215 C'est drôle, mais tu as l'impression que tu as
vu cette Peugeot quelque part[28]. Oui, mais
où? Tu ne te souviens pas. Tu inspectes de
près la Peugeot. Tiens, c'est bizarre. Les roues
sont blanches. Sur le capot[29], il y a un masque
220 de ski. Tu regardes à l'intérieur. Sur le siège
arrière[30], il y a un talkie-walkie. Tu es vraiment
très intrigué(e).

Qu'est-ce que tu feras?

- Tu ouvriras la porte de la Peugeot et
225 tu prendras le talkie-walkie.   **Va au** 107

- Tu prendras le masque de ski.   **Va au** 40

- Tu prendras une photo de
la Peugeot.   **Va au** 40

40 LE ROND-POINT

La pluie a cessé de tomber maintenant. Tu
230 peux **ôter** ton imper, remonter sur ton vélo
et continuer ta promenade. Tu regardes ta
montre. Oh là là, il est six heures du soir. Tu
es pressé(e) de rentrer chez toi, et puis tu
commences à être fatigué(e).

---

[28] somewhere   [29] hood   [30] back seat

MOTS CLÉS
ôter to take off

235 Tu arrives à un rond-point[31]. Il y a trois possibilités pour rentrer chez toi. Tu peux prendre l'autoroute[32] A3. Le problème, c'est qu'il y a toujours beaucoup de circulation[33]. Tu peux prendre la route du nord[34]. C'est une

240 petite route pittoresque avec un café où tu peux t'arrêter. Le problème, c'est que cette route n'est pas en très bon état[35]. Tu peux prendre la route du sud. Le problème, c'est que cette route n'est pas très intéressante.

245 **Quelle route choisiras-tu?**

- Tu prendras l'autoroute A3.   **Va au ⟨108⟩**

- Tu choisiras la route du nord.   **Va au ⟨109⟩**

- Tu prendras la route du sud.   **Va au ⟨110⟩**

⟨100⟩

Ce n'est pas chez toi que tu trouveras le trésor.

250 **Retourne au ⟨11⟩ et choisis une autre option.**

⟨101⟩

Tu n'as pas de chance. Quand tu arriveras au restaurant, tu verras une pancarte qui dit: «Fermé le samedi».

Retourne au ⟨10⟩ et choisis une autre option.

---

[31] traffic circle   [32] toll road
[33] traffic   [34] northern route
[35] in good shape (condition)

255 Fais attention! Ne monte pas sur cette échelle. Elle n'est pas solide. Si tu montais, tu risquerais de tomber et de te casser[36] le cou. Qui viendrait à ton secours?

Choisis une autre option: 22 ou 25

260 Mais pourquoi est-ce que tu as ouvert le placard? À l'intérieur, il y a un squelette[37]! Oui, un squelette humain!

Vraiment, tu as très peur! Tu sautes par la fenêtre[38]. Tu montes sur ton vélo et tu quittes
265 la maison à toute vitesse.

Va au 30

(Ne t'inquiète pas. Le squelette que tu as vu est un squelette utilisé dans les laboratoires d'école. L'ancien propriétaire de la maison
270 était en effet un professeur d'anatomie qui, pour des raisons inconnues[39], gardait[40] ce squelette dans le placard de sa cuisine.)

---

[36] to break   [37] skeleton   [38] window
[39] unknown   [40] kept

Tu as eu une bonne intuition. Après quelques mètres, tu trouves une porte. Cette porte est
275 ouverte. Elle donne dans une petite salle. Avec ta lampe de poche, tu regardes l'intérieur de la salle. Dans un coin[41] il y a trois sacs.

Tu prends un sac. Oh là là, il est lourd! Qu'est-ce qu'il y a dedans? Tu regardes avec
280 ta lampe. Il y a des pièces[42] de métal jaune. Est-ce que tu as découvert le trésor?

Attends! L'histoire n'est pas finie! Tu prends quelques pièces que tu mets dans ton sac à dos. Tu sors de la cave et tu continues ta
285 promenade à vélo.

Va au 30

~~~~~~~~~~~~~~~~~~~~

Ne va pas sous l'arbre. Tu sais bien qu'il est très dangereux de se mettre sous un arbre quand il y a un orage!

290 **Retourne au 30 et choisis une autre option.**

---

[41] corner   [42] coins

Tu vas vers la ferme. Quand tu arrives à la ferme, tu vois un énorme chien. C'est un berger allemand[43]. Bien sûr, il est attaché avec une chaîne, mais il a l'air très, très féroce.

295 Fais demi-tour[44] et va dans la grange.

Va au 31

Ça, vraiment, ce n'est pas une bonne idée. D'abord, c'est illégal de prendre quelque chose qui n'est pas à soi[45]. Et puis, la Peugeot
300 est équipée d'un système d'alarme. Si tu ouvrais la porte, tu déclencherais ce système d'alarme.

Retourne au 31 et choisis une autre option.

Oh là là! Qu'est-ce que c'est? Oh là là, mon
305 Dieu! C'est une voiture de la gendarmerie[46]. Ne sais-tu pas qu'il est absolument **interdit** de circuler à vélo sur une autoroute? Tu dois payer une amende[47] de 50 euros et retourner au rond-point.

310 **Retourne au 40 et choisis une autre option.**

---

[43] German shepherd   [44] turn around   [45] that doesn't belong to you
[46] police   [47] fine

MOTS CLÉS
interdit forbidden, illegal

C'est vrai, cette route est en mauvais état. Ta roue[48] avant heurte une pierre[49] très pointue[50] et tu as une crevaison[51]. Impossible de réparer ta roue. Tu n'as pas les outils[52] nécessaires.
315 Tu dois faire de l'auto-stop[53]. Heureusement, un automobiliste généreux s'arrête et t'amène directement chez toi. (Et il a même[54] la **gentillesse** d'embarquer ton vélo dans son coffre[55].)

320 **Va à** 200 ARRIVÉ

C'est vrai, cette route n'est pas très pittoresque, mais elle est en bon état et il n'y a pas beaucoup de circulation. Tu arrives chez toi fatigué(e) mais content(e) de ta journée.

325 **Va à** 200 ARRIVÉ

260 ARRIVÉE

Tu es enfin chez toi! Qu'est-ce que tu vas faire maintenant? D'abord, tu vas prendre un bain[56]. Ensuite, tu vas dîner. Pendant le dîner, tu racontes les détails de ta journée à ta famille.
330 Après le dîner, tu ouvres ton sac à dos et tu vérifies la liste de tous les objets que tu as trouvés et de toutes les photos que tu as prises.

[48] wheel	[49] stone	[50] sharp	[51] flat tire	[52] tools
[53] hitch-hike	[54] even	[55] trunk	[56] bath	

MOTS CLÉS
la gentillesse kindness

Discovering French, Nouveau! Level 2

OBJETS	PHOTOS
• clé	• photo du lac
• enveloppe	• photo de la maison

Est-ce qu'il y a les choses suivantes sur ta liste?

335   • le billet de loterie?

       • les pièces de métal jaune?

       • la photo de la Peugeot?

• Si tu n'as trouvé aucune
de ces choses,   **Va au** ⟨300⟩

340 • Si tu as le billet de loterie,   **Va au** ⟨301⟩

• Si tu as les pièces,   **Va au** ⟨302⟩

• Si tu as la photo de la Peugeot,   **Va au** ⟨400⟩

〰〰〰〰〰〰〰

 ⟨300⟩

Tu as fait une belle promenade, mais tu n'as
rien trouvé de très intéressant. Si tu veux
345 découvrir le trésor, recommence ta promenade
demain matin.

Retourne à ⎹O DÉPART⎸ et essaie de trouver
les trois choses de la liste.

À la fin de ta promenade,   **Va au** ⟨400⟩

〰〰〰〰〰〰〰

◇ 301

350 On ne gagne pas souvent quand on joue à la loterie. Mais aujourd'hui, tu as de la chance. Le billet de loterie que tu as trouvé gagne 200 euros. (C'est beaucoup d'argent, mais ce n'est pas le trésor.)

355 • Si tu as aussi les pièces, **Va au** ◇ 302

• Si tu as aussi la photo
de la Peugeot, **Va au** ◇ 400

• Si tu as seulement le billet de loterie, retourne demain matin au ▢ 20 et
360 cherche les deux choses que tu n'as pas rapportées de ta promenade.

Continue ta promenade jusqu'à ▢ 200 ARRIVÉE

Va ensuite au ◇ 400

〰〰〰〰〰〰〰〰〰〰

◇ 302

Qu'est-ce que c'est que ce métal jaune? Est-ce
365 que c'est de l'or? Mais non, c'est du cuivre[57]. Et ces pièces de cuivre ne sont pas très anciennes. Leur **valeur**? À peu près 100 euros. Ce n'est pas le trésor.

• Si tu as aussi la photo
370 de la Peugeot,

• Si tu n'as pas la photo, **retourne au** ▢ 30

---

[57] copper

MOTS CLÉS
la valeur value

Discovering French, Nouveau! Level 2

Prends la photo et continue ta promenade jusqu'à $\boxed{\text{200 ARRIVÉE}}$

Va ensuite au **400**

~~~~~~~~~~

Tu as eu raison de prendre la photo de la
375 Peugeot. Évidemment, ce n'est pas le trésor.
Mais c'est la clé du trésor.

Souviens-toi! Quand tu es entré(e) dans la
grange, tu as eu la vague impression d'avoir
vu cette Peugeot quelque part. Après le dîner,
380 tu as montré les photos que tu avais prises à
ta soeur. Elle, elle a reconnu immédiatement
la Peugeot. La photo était en première page
du journal de samedi. C'est la voiture utilisée
par le célèbre gangster Jo Lagachette quand
385 il a attaqué la Banque Populaire la semaine
dernière. Tu sais où il a caché la voiture. Tu
peux apporter ce renseignement à la police.
Elle va arrêter le gangster et toi, tu vas gagner
la prime[58] offerte par la Banque Populaire:
390 20,000 euros. Ça, c'est le trésor!

---

[58] reward

CHALLENGE Once you've completed one version of the bike ride, try again, this time taking another route. How were the two trips different? **(Compare and contrast)**

Vocabulaire de la lecture

Mots clés

rapporter *to bring back*

mener *to lead*

avouer *to admit*

le paysage *landscape, scenery*

ôter *to take off*

interdit *forbidden, illegal*

la gentillesse *kindness*

la valeur *value*

le nord *north*

le sud *south*

A. Écrivez le mot clé dont le sens *(whose meaning)* est le plus proche *(closest)* du contraire du mot donné.

1. suivre _____

2. mettre _____

3. renvoyer *(to send away)* _____

4. permis _____

5. mentir *(to lie)* _____

B. Faites des phrases en utilisant chacun des mots clés suivants: **le paysage, la gentillesse, la valeur, le nord, le sud.**

1. _____

2. _____

3. _____

4. _____

5. _____

Tu as compris?

1. Comment est-ce qu'on va faire la promenade pour finir la chasse au trésor?

_____

2. Qu'est-ce que la météo annonce?

_____

3. Qu'est-ce qu'on met dans le sac à dos?

_____

_____

4. À midi, combien de kilomètres avais-tu fait?

_____

5. Où est-ce qu'on s'arrête d'abord?

_____

Connexion personnelle

Using the notebook to the right, write a short description of a bike ride you took—real or imaginary—in your own neighborhood.

Une randonnée à vélo

Avant de lire   *Quelle soirée!*

Reading Strategy

FOLLOW THE PLOT Use a chart to help you follow what happens in the play. Show what happens in the beginning, middle, and end of the play. What does Olivier do at each point?

Acte 1	Acte 2	Acte 3

What You Need To Know

This is a play in three acts. Each act is divided up into a few scenes. The play focuses on Olivier, a young French man, who, like many young people, wants to impress a girl he likes and take her to a very popular concert. Plays are different from other readings in that much of the action is conveyed by dialogue. Some of the scenes in *Quelle soirée!* are comprised of mainly dialogue and others, narrative, which might involve Olivier delivering monologues onstage if the play were to be dramatized. Usually, narrative sections of plays are meant to convey information to the audience that the characters don't know, but in this play, we don't know more than Olivier, and so we learn along with him.

QUELLE SOIRÉE!

Drame en trois actes

Personnages:

Olivier

Caroline

Jean-Jacques, *cousin d'Olivier*

Monsieur Jamet, *père d'Olivier*

Madame Jamet, *mère d'Olivier*

Acte 1: Olivier trouve une solution

Scène 1

Aujourd'hui, c'est samedi. Olivier est très content. Ce matin il a fait la queue pendant trois heures devant le Rex-Palace. Finalement il a obtenu les deux derniers billets pour le
5 grand concert de ce soir. La seule[1] question est de savoir qui il va inviter…

___
[1] only

READER'S SUCCESS STRATEGY When you form mental images as you read, you are visualizing. This can help you understand and enjoy what you're reading. Listen to the audio and think about how hearing the voices might affect your mental image. Do you form a picture in your mind of the characters?
Jot down some words to describe Olivier and Caroline.

Olivier

Caroline

Olivier pense à Caroline. Caroline est une fille très sympathique et très jolie. Voilà justement le problème. Elle a des quantités d'admirateurs et, par conséquent, beaucoup d'invitations. Est-ce qu'elle sera libre ce soir? Olivier décide de **tenter sa chance.** Il téléphone à Caroline.

10

OLIVIER: Allô, Caroline?

15 CAROLINE: Ah, c'est toi, Olivier? Ça va?

OLIVIER: Ça va! Tu sais, j'ai pu obtenir des billets pour le concert de ce soir.

CAROLINE: Comment as-tu fait? J'ai
20 téléphoné au Rex-Palace. Tout est vendu! Impossible de trouver des billets! Je voulais absolument aller à ce concert.

OLIVIER: Si tu veux, je t'invite.

25 CAROLINE: Tu es vraiment gentil de m'inviter. Bien sûr, j'accepte avec plaisir.

OLIVIER: Bon! Je viendrai te chercher chez toi à huit heures! D'accord?

30 CAROLINE: D'accord! À ce soir!

Scène 2

En rentrant chez lui, Olivier pense au rendez-vous de ce soir. Évidemment, il y a un petit problème. Il a promis à Caroline de venir la chercher chez elle. Oui, mais comment?

MOTS CLÉS
tenter sa chance to try one's luck

Discovering French, Nouveau! Level 2

35 «Heureusement, pense Olivier, il y a la voiture de Papa! Papa est toujours très généreux. Il me prête souvent sa voiture quand j'en ai besoin. Je suis sûr qu'il me la prêtera ce soir.»

Quand il est rentré à la maison, Olivier a tout 40 de suite remarqué que son père **était de très mauvaise humeur.**

OLIVIER: Dis, Papa. Est-ce que je peux prendre ta voiture?

M. JAMET: Pour aller où?

45 OLIVIER: Je voudrais sortir avec une copine.

M. JAMET: Écoute, Olivier, je veux bien que tu sortes, mais je ne veux pas que tu prennes la voiture!

50 OLIVIER: Mais, tu sais que je suis toujours très prudent.

M. JAMET: Je ne veux absolument pas que tu prennes la voiture ce soir. Un point, c'est tout! Si tu veux 55 sortir, tu peux prendre le bus!

OLIVIER: Mais…

M. JAMET: Vraiment, il est inutile que tu insistes.

Scène 3

Olivier est **déçu,** très déçu. Il comptait en 60 effet sur la voiture de son père. C'est une voiture de sport toute neuve. Caroline aurait certainement été² très impressionnée³… Dommage!

---

² would have been   ³ impressed

MOTS CLÉS
être de mauvaise humeur to be in a bad mood
déçu(e) disappointed

Olivier, cependant, ne **perd** pas tout **espoir.**

65 Il sait que ses parents sortent ce soir. Ils sont invités chez les Roussel, des voisins. Olivier sait aussi que lorsque ses parents rendent visite aux Roussel, ils ne rentrent jamais avant une heure du matin.

70 Olivier réfléchit… Le concert finira vers onze heures et demie. Vers minuit il sera de retour chez lui. Ses parents rentreront beaucoup plus tard. Alors?

Alors, Olivier n'hésite plus. Il attend 75 patiemment le départ de ses parents. Puis, à huit heures moins le quart, il prend les clés de la voiture et va dans le garage… Il monte dans la voiture de son père et sort sans faire de bruit… À huit heures, Olivier est chez 80 Caroline.

Acte 2: Olivier a des problèmes
Scène 1

Le concert a commencé à huit heures et demie. L'orchestre est excellent. Caroline est **ravie** et Olivier est très heureux et très **fier** d'être avec elle.

MOTS CLÉS
perdre l'espoir to lose hope   **fier (fière)** proud
ravi(e) delighted

Discovering French, Nouveau! Level 2

85 Soudain, Olivier pense à quelque chose. «Zut,
j'ai oublié d'éteindre⁴ les phares⁵ de la voiture!
Bon, ça ne fait rien⁶. Je vais aller les éteindre
pendant l'entracte⁷.»

À dix heures, l'entracte commence. Olivier dit
90 à Caroline de l'attendre cinq minutes. Il va au
parking où il a laissé la voiture. Là, il a une
très, très mauvaise surprise! Olivier remarque
en effet que le feu arrière de la voiture de son
père est complètement défoncé⁸.

95 «Zut, alors! Pendant que j'étais avec Caroline,
quelqu'un est rentré dans⁹ la voiture de Papa!
Quelle catastrophe! Qu'est-ce que je vais faire?
Il faut que je trouve quelqu'un pour changer
le feu arrière! Oui, mais qui va réparer la
100 voiture maintenant? À cette heure, tous les
garages sont fermés… Il faut absolument que
je trouve une solution! Il faut absolument que
cette voiture soit réparée avant demain matin,
sinon…¹⁰»

Scène 2

105 Olivier pense à son cousin Jean-Jacques.
Jean-Jacques est mécanicien. Il a peut-être les
pièces¹¹ nécessaires. Olivier lui téléphone. Une
voix légèrement irritée répond.

JEAN-JACQUES: Allô…

110   OLIVIER: Jean-Jacques? Il faut que tu
                   m'aides.

---

⁴ turn off	⁵ headlights	⁶ that doesn't matter
⁷ intermission	⁸ smashed in	⁹ ran into
¹⁰ if not	¹¹ parts	

JEAN-JACQUES: Ah, c'est toi, Olivier? Qu'est-ce qui se passe[12]?

OLIVIER: Un accident!

115 JEAN-JACQUES: Grave[13]?

OLIVIER: Je ne sais pas. Quelqu'un est rentré dans la voiture de Papa.

JEAN-JACQUES: Et c'est pour ça que tu me téléphones? Dis donc, je suis
120 en train de regarder un film à la télé. Tu peux bien attendre lundi.

OLIVIER: Non, non! Il faut que tu répares la voiture.

125 JEAN-JACQUES: Dis! Tu ne sais pas qu'on est samedi soir?

OLIVIER: Écoute, c'est très sérieux.

Olivier a expliqué toute la situation: le refus de son père, sa **désobéissance,** le concert,
130 l'accident.

JEAN-JACQUES: Bon, bon! J'ai compris! Si tu veux que je **répare** ta voiture avant le retour de tes parents, il faut que tu viennes
135 immédiatement.

OLIVIER: Merci, Jean-Jacques! Tu es un vrai copain!

---

[12] What's up?   [13] serious

MOTS CLÉS
désobéir to disobey

réparer to repair

Scène 3

Maintenant Olivier est rassuré, mais il est aussi inquiet[14]. Il faut qu'il aille chez Jean-
₁₄₀ Jacques immédiatement! Est-ce que Caroline comprendra la situation? Olivier retourne au concert… C'est la fin[15] de l'entracte.

CAROLINE: Dis, Olivier, où étais-tu? Je commençais à m'impatienter…

₁₄₅ OLIVIER: Excuse-moi!… Euh… Il faut que je te raccompagne chez toi…

CAROLINE: Mais le concert n'est pas fini.

OLIVIER: Il faut absolument que je rentre.

₁₅₀ CAROLINE: Tu es malade?

OLIVIER: Euh, non… Il faut que j'aille chez mon cousin qui est garagiste.

CAROLINE: Comment? Il faut que tu ailles
₁₅₅ chez le garagiste à dix heures du soir? Si tu n'es pas malade, tu es fou!

OLIVIER: Je suis vraiment désolé, mais il faut que je parte…

₁₆₀ CAROLINE: Eh bien, moi, je suis furieuse que tu me traites de cette façon[16]! Veux-tu que je te dise quelque chose? Tu es un vrai mufle[17]! Et la prochaine fois,
₁₆₅ il est inutile que tu m'invites. Après tout, j'ai d'autres copains!

---

[14] worried [15] end
[16] like that [17] a real clod (jerk)

CHALLENGE Do you think Caroline was right to be angry with Olivier? Why or why not? **(Make Judgments)**

Acte 3: Sauvé? Pas tout à fait!
Scène 1

Olivier a raccompagné Caroline chez elle.
Il arrive chez son cousin. Il est onze heures
170 maintenant. Jean-Jacques examine la voiture.

OLIVIER: Alors?

JEAN-JACQUES: Il faut que je répare le pare-
chocs et que je change le feu
arrière.

175 OLIVIER: Ce n'est pas trop sérieux?

JEAN-JACQUES: Non, mais tu as de la chance
que j'aie les pièces de
rechange[18].

Jean-Jacques est un excellent mécanicien.
180 À minuit, il a fini la réparation[19]. Olivier
remercie son cousin et rentre chez lui…

Scène 2

Olivier est arrivé chez lui à minuit et demi.
Ses parents sont rentrés bien plus tard, vers
une heure et demie. Ils n'ont rien remarqué…

185 Olivier s'est couché immédiatement après son

---

[18] spare part   [19] repair

retour, mais il n'a pas pu dormir. Il pense aux
événements de la soirée.

«Quelle soirée! Elle avait si bien[20] commencé.
Et puis, il y a eu cet accident ridicule!
190 Heureusement Jean-Jacques était chez lui!
Est-ce que Papa **s'apercevra de** la réparation?
Non! Jean-Jacques est un excellent mécanicien
et Papa est un peu myope[21]. Il ne s'apercevra
de rien… Sinon, ce serait un drame à la
195 maison!

«Et Caroline? Elle était vraiment furieuse!
Bah, tant pis[22]! L'essentiel c'est que la voiture
soit réparée.

Je suis **sauvé,** sauvé… »

Scène 3

200 Dimanche matin, Olivier s'est levé assez tard.
Il a trouvé sa mère dans la cuisine. Madame
Jamet est en train de préparer le déjeuner.

Mme Jamet: Tu sais, Olivier, il ne faut
pas que tu sois fâché contre[23]
205 ton père. S'il ne t'a pas prêté
sa voiture hier, c'est qu'il
y avait une raison. Il faut
que je t'explique ce qui s'est
passé[24]. Hier matin, comme
210 tous les samedis, ton père est
allé faire les courses. Pendant

---

[20] so well	[21] nearsighted
[22] too bad	[23] angry with, upset with
[24] what happened	

MOTS CLÉS
s'apercevoir de   to notice   **sauvé(e)**   saved

1. Which of the following best describes the moral of the story? **(Main Idea)**

_____ Never borrow your father's car.

_____ It's best not to invite a pretty girl out on a date.

_____ Honesty is the best policy.

_____ Father knows best.

_____ It is best not to hire family members.

2. If you had been in Olivier's situation, what would you have done? **(Connect)**

qu'il était au supermarché, quelqu'un est rentré dans sa voiture. Évidemment, le type[25] qui a fait ça est parti sans laisser de trace. Il paraît que le pare-chocs et le feu arrière sont endommagés[26]! Quand Papa est rentré à la maison, il était absolument furieux. Il était si furieux qu'il n'a rien dit à personne. Enfin, il s'est calmé et chez les Roussel il a tout raconté. Tu t'imagines[27]? Une voiture toute neuve[28]! Tu comprends maintenant pourquoi il n'a pas voulu te prêter la voiture hier soir!

Épilogue

À cause de l'accident, Olivier est dans une situation très embarrassante. Selon vous, quelle est la meilleure solution?

- Il faut qu'il prenne un marteau[29] et qu'il casse à nouveau le feu arrière de la voiture.
- Il faut qu'il propose à son père de réparer lui-même la voiture.
- Il faut qu'il dise la vérité.

Avez-vous une autre solution à proposer à Olivier?

[25] guy   [26] damaged   [27] Can you imagine?
[28] brand-new   [29] hammer

Vocabulaire de la lecture

Mots clés

tenter sa chance *to try one's luck*	**fier (fière)** *proud*
être de mauvaise humeur *to be in a bad mood*	**désobéir** *to disobey*
déçu(e) *disappointed*	**réparer** *to repair*
perdre l'espoir *to lose hope*	**s'apercevoir de** *to notice*
ravi(e) *delighted*	**sauvé(e)** *saved*

A. Mettez en regard le mot clé à gauche et son synonyme à droite.

_____ **1.** désobéir

_____ **2.** réparer

_____ **3.** ravi(e)

_____ **4.** s'apercevoir de

_____ **5.** perdre l'espoir

a. discerner *(to perceive)*

b. transgresser *(to go against)*

c. ne plus avoir confiance

d. enchanté(e)

e. estaurer; refaire *(restore)*

B. Faites un paragraphe qui décrit une mésaventure en utilisant au moins quatre des mots clés.

_____

_____

_____

_____

_____

_____

Tu as compris?

1. Pourquoi est-ce qu'Olivier est très content au début?

_____

2. Dans Scène 2, Olivier a un petit problème. Qu'est-ce que c'est?

_____

3. Qu'est-ce qu'Olivier a découvert pendant l'entracte?

_____

4. Pourquoi est-ce qu'il faut réparer la voiture tout de suite?

_____

_____

5. À la fin, est-ce qu'Olivier est vraiment sauvé?

_____

Connexion personnelle

Imagine the conversation between Olivier and Caroline as he drives her home from the concert in the beginning of Acte 3, Scène 1. Use dashes to indicate dialogue.

Dans la voiture...

Lectures supplémentaires

In this section you will find literary readings in French. Like the **Interludes** readings, the literary readings have reading strategies, reading tips, reader's success strategies, critical-thinking questions, vocabulary activities, comprehension questions, and a short writing activity to help you understand each selection. There is also an **À Marquer** feature for literary analysis of the readings.

Avant de lire   *Le chat (extrait)*

Reading Strategy

OBSERVE WHAT MAKES POETRY Poetry is a form of literature—a piece of imaginative writing—organized in a particular way that emphasizes rhythm and sound. Answer the following questions to observe the characteristics of rhyme and rhythm in this poem.

RHYTHM Read the poem out aloud. Can you tap a steady beat?

_____

RHYME Pay attention to the sounds of the last word of each line. Is there a pattern? Write the words that rhyme here:

_____

_____

What You Need To Know

The word poetry comes from the Greek *poesis,* which means *making* or *creating.* Poetry differs from prose in the way that it is organized. While prose is organized in sentences and paragraphs, poetry is organized in *lines* and *stanzas* (the "paragraphs" of poetry). Poems express feelings, capture moments, and reveal the essence of life. *Le chat* appeared in *Les Fleurs du mal* (1857), Charles Baudelaire's most famous book and collection of poetry.

À propos de l'auteur

Charles Baudelaire est un des poètes les plus importants de la littérature française. Il est né en 1821 à Paris. Il a publié *Les Fleurs du mal* en 1857. C'est un livre qui rassemble la plupart *(most)* de ses oeuvres *(works)* précédentes. Baudelaire s'intéresse aux idées du bien et du mal *(good and evil)* et à la beauté, et à la vie parisienne. Il est mort *(died)* en 1867.

Le chat

Dans ma cervelle[1] se promène,

Ainsi qu[2]'en son appartement,

Un beau chat, **fort, doux** et **charmant.**

Quand il miaule[3], on l'entend à peine[4],

5   Tant son timbre[5] est **tendre** et **discret;**

Mais que sa voix s'apaise[6] ou gronde[7],

Elle est toujours **riche** et **profonde.**

C'est là son charme et son secret.

De sa fourrure[8] blonde et brune

10   Sort un **parfum** si doux qu'un soir

J'en fus embaumé[9], pour l'avoir

Caressée une fois, rien qu'une[10].

C'est l'esprit[11] familier du lieu;

Il juge, il préside, il inspire

15   Toutes choses dans son empire;

Peut-être est-il fée[12], est-il dieu[13]?

---

[1] brain [2] just as [3] meows [4] hardly [5] timber, tone
[6] appeases [7] complains [8] fur [9] I was perfumed by it
[10] only once [11] spirit [12] fairy [13] a god

MOTS CLÉS
fort(e) strong
doux / douce gentle
charmant(e) charming
tendre tender

discret / discrète unassuming, unobtrusive
riche rich
profond(e) deep
un parfum scent

À réfléchir…

In what way is the cat in the poem like most cats? **(Infer)**

À MARQUER **ANALYSE LITTÉRAIRE Alliteration** is the repetition of the same vowel or consonant sounds, to give the poem a musical sense. Read the boxed text and underline an example of alliteration.

READING TIP Always read poetry out loud. Let the punctuation tell you where to stop and pause—not the line and stanza breaks.

READER'S SUCCESS STRATEGY Underline all the adjectives you come across in the poem. Some French adjectives—like English adjectives—can have double meanings. **Profond** can mean *deep* as in a deep tone of voice, *deep* as in complicated, or *deep* as in deep water.

CHALLENGE What does the poet mean when he says that the cat walks in his brain? **(Draw Conclusions)**

Vocabulaire de la lecture

Mots clés

fort(e) *strong*

doux / douce *gentle*

charmant(e) *charming*

tendre *tender*

discret / discrète *unassuming, unobtrusive*

riche *rich*

profond(e) *deep*

un parfum *scent*

beau *beautiful, handsome*

A. Fill in each blank with the vocabulary word whose meaning is closest to the opposite of the word given.

1. faible _____

2. laid _____

3. sévère _____

4. désagréable _____

5. dur _____

B. Fill in each blank with the appropriate vocabulary word.

1. J'aime le _____ des roses.

2. À l'hôtel, la femme de ménage est très _____; elle arrive et fait son travail sans beaucoup de bruit.

3. Attention si tu vas nager ici! L'eau est très _____.

4. C'est un homme avec beaucoup d'argent; il est assez _____.

Tu as compris?

1. Comment est le chat?

_____

2. Comment est sa voix?

_____

3. De quelle couleur est sa fourrure?

_____

4. Combien de fois est-ce que le narrateur a caressé le chat?

_____

5. Que fait le chat?

_____

Connexion personnelle

Write a description of a special pet, real or imaginary. What kind of animal is it? What does it look like? What does it like to do? Use the notebook to the right to write your description.

Avant de lire   *Gros nuages gris*

Reading Strategy

READ FOR OVERALL MEANING When you read poetry, it's important to read at least once through without stopping in order to get the overall idea. Don't stop, even if there are words or images that confuse you. Use the chart to identify the speaker and the situation of the poem.

DANS LE POÈME...

Qui parle?	
Qu'est-ce qui se passe dans le poème?	

What You Need To Know

Most poems rely on *figurative language* to create meaning. Figurative language refers to language that goes beyond the literal meaning of words, and covers a variety of literary devices known as *figures of speech.* One such figure of speech is *metaphor,* a direct comparison of two things that are often *not* alike. By using metaphors, a poet creates a fresh insight or way of seeing in the mind of the reader. *Gros nuages gris* compares the movement of clouds to many activities familiar to the poet, and uses metaphor to describe the act of poetic inspiration.

Discovering French, Nouveau! **Level 2**

Gros nuages gris

Henriette Charasson

— **Gros nuages** gris dans **le ciel** gris, où **courez-**vous si vite ?

— *Nous allons pour aller, nous courons pour courir*

*Comme tes poèmes s'égrènent[1] sous **le vent** qui te visite,*

*Comme tu chantes pour chanter, comme une plante va **fleurir**.*

— Gros nuages gris qui jamais nulle part[2] ne trouverez de gîte[3],

Gros nuages gris dans le ciel gris, où courez-vous si vite,

     Nuages gris?

— *Nous allons pour aller, nous courons pour courir*

*Comme tu vas et chanteras jusqu'à l'heure de **mourir**,*

     Comme tu vis[4],

     Toi qui écris…

— Gros nuages gris dans le ciel gris, où courez-vous si vite?

— *Comme tes poèmes s'égrènent sous le vent qui te visite,*

Nous allons pour aller, nous courons pour courir,

     Nuages gris!

---

[1] ripple out	[2] nowhere
[3] shelter / home	[4] live

MOTS CLÉS

gros(se)	big, large		**le vent**	the wind
un nuage	a cloud		**fleurir**	to flower
le ciel	the sky		**mourir**	to die
courir	to run			

À réfléchir…

Why do the clouds move so fast across the sky? Put a checkmark next to the correct answer. **(Clarify)**

☐ They're running home.

☐ They run for the pleasure of running.

☐ They're trying to escape from someone else.

A MARQUER ▷ **ANALYSE LITTÉRAIRE** A metaphor is a comparison of two things without using the words *like* or *as*. Find an example of metaphor in the poem and underline it. Write it here.

_____

_____

READING TIP Remember that dashes are used to indicate dialogue. In this poem, italics are also used to separate one speaking voice from another.

READER'S SUCCESS STRATEGY Read the poem aloud and as you read, find and circle words at the ends of lines of the poem that rhyme. What pattern do you notice? Write it below.

_____

_____

_____

CHALLENGE Why does the poet want to know where the clouds are going? **(Infer)**

_____

_____

Vocabulaire de la lecture

Mots clés

gros(se) *big, large*

un nuage *a cloud*

le ciel *the sky*

courir *to run*

le vent *the wind*

fleurir *to flower*

mourir *to die*

jamais *never*

une plante *a plant*

A. Fill in each blank with the appropriate vocabulary word.

1. Au printemps, beaucoup de plantes _____.

2. Alain aime aller vite. Il aime _____.

3. Quand il pleut, il y a beaucoup de _____ dans le ciel.

4. Pour faire de la voile, il vaut mieux avoir un peu de _____.

5. Sophie a acheté une jolie _____ pour mettre dans le jardin.

B. Fill in each blank with the vocabulary word whose meaning is closest to the opposite of the word given.

1. toujours   _____

2. petit   _____

3. vivre   _____

4. la terre   _____

Tu as compris?

1. Que font les nuages gris?

_____

2. Qu'est-ce que le poète demande aux nuages?

_____

3. Selon les nuages, comment est-ce que le poète crée ses poèmes?

_____

4. Pourquoi est-ce que les nuages courent?

_____

5. Quand les nuages disent «tu» dans le poème, qui est-ce?

_____

Connexion personnelle

What other questions might you ask clouds if you had the opportunity? Make a list here.

Les nuages

_____

_____

_____

_____

_____

_____

_____

_____

_____

Avant de lire
Alléluia!
Comptine: *Le régiment des fromages blancs*

Reading Strategy

WORD CHOICE Poets choose words in order to elicit specific feelings from readers. In addition to its literal meaning, or *denotation,* most words also have a *connotation…* an implied or associated meaning. For example, the word *turkey* means a type of poultry (that is its literal meaning), but for Americans, *turkey* has come to have an associated meaning of Thanksgiving. Look at the titles of these short pieces and write down some additional words you associate with each title.

Titre	Mots

What You Need To Know

Alléluia is a poem written by Maurice Carême, who is sometimes referred to as the Robert Louis Stevenson of French literature. In *Alléluia,* Carême writes about the holiday of **Mardi Gras** *(Fat Tuesday),* using language to suggest both the religious and secular connotations of the season. *Le régiment des fromages blancs* is a **comptine** that parodies a popular French military song, *Le régiment de Sambre et Meuse,* which was written in the 1870s by Paul Cézano and inspired by the French folk tales of peasant armies during the French Revolution.

À propos de l'auteur

Maurice Carême est né en 1899 à Wavre, en Belgique. Instituteur de 1918 à 1942, il quitte l'enseignement en 1943 pour se consacrer *(dedicate himself)* entièrement à l'écriture. Il a écrit non seulement des poèmes mais aussi des contes, des romans, des essais, et des légendes. Il est plus connu comme écrivain de livres pour des enfants–inspirés peut-être par ses années d'enseignement. Ses autres sujets préférés sont la nature, sa mère (sur laquelle il a beaucoup écrit), et la vie quotidienne *(daily life)*. Il est mort en 1977.

~~~~~~~~~~

Alléluia!

C'est **mardi gras.**

Les **escargots**

S'en vont au trot[1]

Dans les assiettes.

5 Et **les galettes**

Se noient à flot[2]

Dans le sirop.

Alléluia!

Les choux sont gras[3].

10 Il y en a

Pour tous les gars[4]

Dansez fourchettes,

Sautez[5] **noisettes.**

Alléluia!

15 C'est mardi gras.

---

[1] at a trot   [2] drown in the stream (of syrup)
[3] thick, plump   [4] boys / guys   [5] leap

MOTS CLÉS

mardi gras "Fat Tuesday," the day before Ash Wednesday. Typically a day of celebration before the fasting of Lent begins.

un escargot snail
une galette waffle
un chou cabbage
une noisette hazelnut

À réfléchir...

Why does the speaker tell the forks to dance and the hazelnuts to jump? **(Infer)**

_____

_____

⫸ À MARQUER⟫ ANALYSE LITTÉRAIRE *Personification* is giving human qualities to inanimate objects. For example, in *Alléluia!*, waffles are described as drowning. Both the poem and **comptine** make liberal use of personification. Underline examples in both, and explain them here.

_____

_____

_____

_____

_____

READER'S SUCCESS STRATEGY The poet uses food to convey his ideas about **Mardi Gras.** And in the **comptine,** different types of cheese are used to replace people at war with each other. As you read, note all the types of food mentioned. List them here.

_____

_____

_____

_____

Le régiment des fromages blancs

Un régiment
De fromages blancs
Partait en guerre
Contre les camemberts.
5   Le port-salut
N'a pas voulu
Car le roquefort
Puait[6] trop fort.
Le livarot
10   Portait le **drapeau**
Et les petits suisses[7] chantaient La Marseillaise.
Cela faisait un chant nouveau…
La France est belle sous les drapeaux!

[6] smelled, stunk
[7] a kind of cream cheese eaten for dessert, particularly by children

MOTS CLÉS
un drapeau flag

Vocabulaire de la lecture

Mots clés

mardi gras   *"Fat Tuesday," the day before Ash Wednesday. Typically a day of celebration before the fasting of Lent begins.*

un escargot   *snail*

une galette   *waffle*

un chou (des choux)   *cabbage(s)*

une noisette   *hazelnut*

un drapeau   *flag*

une assiette   *plate*

une fourchette   *fork*

un fromage   *cheese*

vouloir   *to wish or want*

A. Écrivez le mot clé qui convient le mieux.

1. Le jour avant Mercredi des cendres *(Ash Wednesday).*   _____

2. On peut le manger pour le petit déjeuner ou pour le dessert.   _____

3. Il est le symbole du pays.   _____

4. Un mollusque qui peut habiter dans l'eau ou dans le jardin.   _____

5. Une sorte de petite noix.   _____

B. Écrivez un petit paragraphe sur un repas en utilisant des mots clés qui restent.

_____

_____

_____

_____

_____

Tu as compris?

1. Dans le poème, quel jour est-ce?

_____

2. Que font les escargots?

_____

3. Combien de choux est-ce qu'il y a?

_____

4. Dans la comptine, qui va en guerre contre les camemberts?

_____

5. Qu'est-ce que les petits suisses chantaient _(were singing)_?

_____

Connexion personnelle

If you had to write a poem about a holiday, what food might you use to describe that holiday? How would you personify the food? Make a list on the notebook.

Avant de lire   *Chanson de la Seine*

Reading Strategy

GETTING AN OVERALL IMPRESSION Read the poem aloud twice. Look up any unfamiliar words and scan the **mots clés.** Use the chart to record your initial impressions. What sticks with you after you read? How would you characterize the *tone?* What words give it that tone?

REPETITION	
TONE	

What You Need To Know

Chanson de la Seine was published in 1951 as part of the collection *Spectacles.* Jacques Prévert often wrote about Paris and Parisian life after World War II. While his poems were usually characterized by optimism and humor, he also took seriously the ideas of liberty and freedom and took issue with bourgeois life and institutions, all of which made their way into his poems. In *Chanson de la Seine,* he uses *personification* to describe both the Seine and Notre Dame.

À réfléchir...

Why do you think the poet doesn't mention misery until the end? **(Draw Conclusion)**

_____

_____

_____

||||À MARQUER>> ANALYSE LITTÉRAIRE As you know, _personification_ is a literary device in which inanimate objects are given human characteristics. Read the boxed text and underline the examples of personification that you find.

READING TIP Sometimes poems do not observe standard writing conventions. Often, for example, each line of a poem starts with a capital letter, even though that line may not be the beginning of a new sentence. Poets are free to establish their own style. In the space below, write two lines from this poem that start with a capital letter and are _not_ new sentences.

_____

_____

_____

_____

_____

À propos de l'auteur

Jacques Prévert est né en 1900 à Neuilly-sur-Seine où il a grandi. En 1920, il s'engage _(joined)_ dans l'armée, où il fait la connaissance d'Yves Tanguy et Marcel Duhamel, avec lesquels il participera au mouvement surréaliste. Prévert a commencé à écrire dans les années 30. Il est l'auteur de poèmes, mais aussi de scénarios de films dont les plus connus sont _Le Crime de M. Lange_ (réalisateur Jean Renoir), et _Les enfants du paradis_ (Marcel Carné). Il est mort en 1977.

Chanson de la Seine

La Seine a de la chance

Elle n'a pas de **soucis**

Elle se la coule douce[1]

Le jour comme la nuit

5   Et elle sort de sa source[2]

Tout **doucement** sans bruit

Et sans se faire de mousse[3]

Sans sortir de son lit

Elle s'en va vers la mer

10   En passant par Paris

> La Seine a de la chance
>
> Elle n'a pas de soucis
>
> Et quand elle se promène[4]
>
> Tout le long[5] de ses **quais**
>
> 15   Avec sa belle robe verte
>
> Et ses **lumières** dorées[6]

---

[1] has it easy   [2] its origin   [3] without getting all worried
[4] walks / takes a walk / ambles   [5] all along   [6] golden

MOTS CLÉS

un souci a worry   **un quai** embankment
doucement gently   **une lumière** light

Discovering French, Nouveau! **Level 2**

Notre-Dame **jalouse**

Immobile et sévère

Du haut de[7] toutes ses pierres

20 La regarde de travers[8]

Mais la Seine s'en balance[9]

Elle n'a pas de soucis

Elle se la coule douce

Le jour comme la nuit

25 Et s'en va vers le Havre

Et s'en va vers la mer .

En passant comme **un rêve**

Au milieu des mystères

Des **misères** de Paris.

---

[7] from on top of   [8] askew   [9] could care less

READER'S SUCCESS STRATEGY The *tone* in a poem is the author's attitude toward his or her subject. Possible attitudes might be pessimistic, humorous, bitter, serious, playful. Usually, an author's tone is revealed through word choice and details. A poem might carry one consistent tone throughout, or the tone might change. As you read through the poem, decide what you think the tone is at the beginning. Does it change? If so, where?

CHALLENGE How do you think the poet feels about life in Paris? Explain. **(Infer)**

MOTS CLÉS
jaloux(-se) jealous
un rêve dream
au milieu des in the middle of

un mystère mystery
la misère misery, misfortune

Vocabulaire de la lecture

Mots clés

un souci *a worry*

doucement *gently*

un quai *embankment*

une lumière *light*

jaloux(-se) *jealous*

un rêve *dream*

au milieu des *in the middle of*

un mystère *mystery*

la misère *misery, misfortune*

A. Décidez si les deux mots constituent des antonymes ou des synonymes.

ANTONYME   SYNONYME

1. un souci – un plaisir   _____   _____

2. jaloux – envieux   _____   _____

3. des misères – des malheurs   _____   _____

4. doucement – brutalement   _____   _____

5. un mystère – une clarté   _____   _____

B. Écrivez quatre phrases en utilisant les mots clés qui restent.

1. _____

2. _____

3. _____

4. _____

Tu as compris?

1. Comment est-ce que la Seine sort de sa source?

_____

2. Où va la Seine?

_____

3. Comment est Notre Dame?

_____

4. Que «porte» la Seine?

_____

5. Qu'est-ce qui regarde la Seine de travers?

_____

Connexion personnelle

Imagine you are writing a poem about something in nature—a river, mountain, beach, field, etc. How would you personify it? What mood would you convey? Make a list of French words and phrases that you would use to describe your place. Write your list of descriptive words in the notebook at the right.

Avant de lire

Les dromadaires
Le bonheur

Reading Strategy

USE CONTEXT TO DETERMINE MEANING Even though these readings are brief, there might be many unfamiliar words. Scan the two poems and see if you can find words that mean the following:

roamed _____

to leave _____

apple tree _____

cherry tree _____

What You Need To Know

Poems can serve several functions. They can be examples of the finest literary writing, inspiring readers and listeners by their use of language, their word choice, and their unique form of expression. Poems can tell a story, capture one moment, or reveal a truth. They can be playful and silly; they can make us laugh. Poems don't always have to be serious to be successful, and they can be enjoyed by anyone, at any age.

À propos de l'auteur

Guillaume Apollinaire–Wilhelm Apollinaris de Kostrowitsky–est né à Rome d'une mère polonaise et d'un père italien. Il a passé sa jeunesse *(youth)* en France sur la Côte d'Azur, et en 1889, il démenage *(moved)* à Paris où il passera le reste de sa vie sauf *(except)* deux ans à l'étranger. Il est connu surtout comme poète lyrique mais il est également l'auteur de critiques d'art. Les plus grands sujets de sa poésie sont l'amour, la nostalgie de la jeunesse, et la solitude. Il est mort en 1960.

~~~~~~~~~

Les dromadaires

Avec ses quatre **dromadaires,**
don Pedro d'Alfaroubeira
courut[1] le monde et l'**admira;**
il fit[2] ce que je voudrais faire
5 si j'avais quatre dromadaires.

---

[1] roamed   [2] he did

À réfléchir...

1. How would you describe the tone of the two poems? **(Evaluate)**

2. What does the poets' use of language suggest about audience? **(Draw Conclusions)**

READING TIP Note that both of these poems have verbs in the **passé simple,** which is the literary past tense: **courut (courir), admira (admirer),** and **fit (faire).**

READER'S SUCCESS STRATEGY After you read through the poems (at least once out loud), make note of any figures of speech and other techniques you notice in the poems. What effects do they cause?

MOTS CLÉS
un dromadaire camel
admirer (admira = passé simple) to admire

▐▐▐ À MARQUER⧽ ANALYSE LITTÉRAIRE Repetition is a literary technique in which words and phrases are repeated for emphasis or unity. In *Le bonheur*, circle the phrase that is repeated throughout. How does it function?

CHALLENGE Do you think a meadow is an appropriate place to find happiness? Why or why not? **(Evaluate)**

À propos de l'auteur

Paul Fort est poète et dramaturge. Il est né à Reims en 1872. En 1905, il fonde la revue *Vers et Prose* avec un autre poète, Paul Valéry, dans laquelle ils publient des oeuvres des écrivains les plus importants de l'époque, comme Apollinaire. On l'a appelé "le prince des poètes." Fort est mort en 1960.

Le bonheur

Le bonheur est dans **le pré,**
      cours-y-vite, cours-y-vite!
Le bonheur est dans le pré,
      cours-y-vite, il va **filer!**

5 Si tu veux le **rattraper,**
      cours-y-vite, cours-y-vite!
Si tu veux le rattraper,
      cours-y-vite, il va filer!

De **pommier** en **cerisier,**
10   cours-y-vite, cours-y-vite!
De pommier en cerisier,
      cours-y-vite, il va filer!

Saute par-dessus[3] **la haie,**
      cours-y-vite, cours-y-vite!
15 Saute par-dessus la haie,
      cours-y-vite, il va filer!

_____
[3] over the top of

MOTS CLÉS

le bonheur happiness
le pré meadow
filer to go / fly off
rattraper to catch up with

un pommier an apple tree
un cerisier a cherry tree
la haie the hedge

Vocabulaire de la lecture

Mots clés

un dromadaire *camel*

admirer *to admire*

le bonheur *happiness*

le pré *meadow*

filer *to go / fly off*

rattraper *to catch up with*

un pommier *apple tree*

un cerisier *cherry tree*

la haie *hedge*

courir *to run*

A. Choisissez la meilleure définition pour chaque mot.

_____ **1.** un pommier

_____ **2.** le bonheur

_____ **3.** la haie

_____ **4.** un cerisier

_____ **5.** un dromadaire

a. une série de petits arbres qui sont ensemble pour limiter ou protéger un champ ou un jardin

b. un arbre dont le fruit est une pomme

c. le sentiment qui exprime que l'on est content

d. un animal qui habite dans le désert

d. un arbre dont le fruit est une cerise

B. Faites quatre phrases en utilisant les mots clés qui restent.

1. _____

2. _____

3. _____

4. _____

5. _____

Tu as compris?

1. Combien de dromadaires a don Pedro d'Alfaroubeira?

_____

2. Qu'est-ce qu'il a fait avec ses dromadaires?

_____

3. Pourquoi est-ce que le narrateur du poème _Les dromadaires_ ne court pas le monde?

_____

4. Où est le bonheur?

_____

5. Pourquoi est-ce qu'il faut courir vite?

_____

Connexion personnelle

We run after and chase both literal things (the bus, a pickpocket), and abstract things (time, dreams, etc.). Make a list on the notebook to the right of those things you might run after or chase.

Je cours après...

Avant de lire   *La rue de Bagnolet*
Coccinelle

Reading Strategy

CLARIFY THE MEANING OF A POEM The process of stopping while reading to quickly review what has happened and to look for answers to questions you may have is called *clarifying*. Complete the chart below by doing the following:

- Divide *La rue de Bagnolet* into six sections (the length of the sections may vary).
- Read the first section.
- Stop to clarify that section.
- Paraphrase what that section is about below.
- Continue to read and clarify the other five sections of the poem in the same manner.

_____

_____

_____

_____

_____

_____

What You Need To Know

This reading includes the poems *La rue de Bagnolet* by Robert Desnos (1900–1945) and *Coccinelle* by Edmond Rostand (1868–1918). Both poems talk about the sun, often a symbol in poetry of happiness, joy, and light. Both of these poems mention home—though in *La rue de Bagnolet,* the poem refers indirectly to this concept.

À réfléchir...

1. How would you describe the tone of both poems? **(Make Judgments)**

_____

_____

_____

2. Why does the poet say that the sun from the rue de Bagnolet isn't like any other sun? **(Draw Conclusions)**

_____

_____

_____

_____

_____

_____

⫯ À MARQUER⟩ ANALYSE LITTÉRAIRE The poet's choice of words is called _diction_. Look at the diction in both poems and underline the words that contribute to the overall tone of the poems.

READING TIP You've already learned several reflexive verbs. As you read both of these poems, circle the reflexive verbs you come across.

À propos de l'auteur

Robert Desnos était un poète français de tradition surréaliste. Il est né à Paris en 1900. Pendant son service militaire, il a fait la connaissance d'André Bréton, avec qui il a pratiqué la technique de l'_écriture automatique_–une méthode d'écriture _(writing)_ qui demande au poète d'entrer en transe hypnotique et d'écrire ce qui sort inconsciemment de son esprit inconscient.

~~~~~~~~~~

La rue de Bagnolet

Le soleil de la rue de Bagnolet

N'est pas un soleil comme les autres[1].

Il **se baigne** dans **le ruisseau,**

Il **se coiffe** avec un seau[2],

5 Tout comme les autres,

Mais, quand il caresse mes épaules

C'est bien lui[3] et pas un autre,

Le soleil de la rue de Bagnolet

Qui **conduit** son cabriolet[4]

10 Ailleurs qu'aux portes **des palais.**

Soleil tout **drôle** et tout content,

Soleil de la rue de Bagnolet,

Pas comme les autres.

---

[1] like the others
[2] a bucket
[3] It's definitely him
[4] convertible

MOTS CLÉS
le soleil   the sun
se baigner   take a bath / bathe
le ruisseau   stream
se coiffer   to style or cut hair

conduire   to drive
un palais   palace
drôle   funny, amusing

À propos de l'auteur

Edmond Rostand était poète et dramaturge. Il est né à Marseille en 1868. Sa première pièce qui a eu du succès a été *Les Romanesques,* qu'il a écrite en 1894, et qui est basée sur *Roméo et Juliette.* Son oeuvre la plus connue est la pièce *Cyrano de Bergerac.* En 1901, Rostand fut *(was)* le plus jeune écrivain élu à l'Académie Française. Il est mort en 1918.

~~~~~~~~~~

Coccinelle

Coccinelle[5], demoiselle

Où t'en vas-tu donc[6]?

Je m'en vais dans le soleil

Car c'est là qu'est ma maison.

5 Bonjour, bonjour, dit le soleil,

Il fait chaud et **il fait bon.**

Le monde est plein **de merveilles**

Il fait bon se lever **tôt.**

---
[5] ladybug   [6] then; so

MOTS CLÉS

il fait bon it's nice out   **tôt** early

une merveille marvel

Vocabulaire de la lecture

Mots clés

le soleil *the sun*

se baigner *take a bath / bathe*

le ruisseau *stream*

se coiffer *to style or cut hair*

conduire *to drive*

un palais *palace*

drôle *funny, amusing*

il fait bon *it's nice out*

une merveille *marvel*

tôt *early*

A. Complétez chaque phrase par le mot clé qui convient le mieux.

1. J'ai les cheveux trop longs. Il faut _____.

2. Quand il fait jour, _____ se lève.

3. Le roi et la reine habitent dans _____.

4. Il y a un petit _____ qui court dans la forêt.

5. Vas-tu nous _____ dans ta nouvelle voiture?

B. Écrivez le mot clé dont le sens est le plus proche du contraire du mot donné.

1. tard _____

2. il fait mauvais _____

3. ennuyeux _____

4. des choses ordinaires _____

5. se salir _____

Tu as compris?

1. Où se baigne le soleil de la rue de Bagnolet?

_____

2. Comment est-ce que le soleil se coiffe?

_____

3. Qu'est-ce que le soleil conduit?

_____

4. Où habite la coccinelle?

_____

5. Dans le poème _Coccinelle,_ quel temps fait-il, selon le soleil?

_____

Connexion personnelle

How might you describe your own childhood neighborhood? Would you use the sun? The light? The smell? Use the notebook on the right to list your ideas.

Avant de lire

Rondeau
Comptine: Je te donne pour ta fête

Reading Strategy

DETERMINE THE RHYTHMICAL DEVICE USED BY THE POET Read the
poem *Rondeau* several times. What is the basic line length? Can you tap
out the number of syllables? How many stanzas are there?

Nombre de syllabes dans chaque ligne	
Nombre de strophes (stanzas)	

What You Need To Know

The poem *Rondeau,* by Charles d'Orléans (1391-1465), is a version of a
rondeau or **rondel,** a closed-form of French medieval poetry. Typically, a
rondel is comprised of thirteen lines, divided into 3 stanzas and using only
2 rhymes. Typically, too, the stanzas of the **rondel** are grouped according to
the following rhyme scheme: A B B A; A B 12 (the repetition or **rentrement**
of the first two lines); A B B A 1. Many **rondels** are songs of love and spring.

À propos de l'auteur

Charles d'Orléans est généralement désigné le père de la poésie lyrique française. Il était le petit-fils du roi Charles V, et le père de Louis XII. En 1415, il a été capturé pendant la bataille d'Agincourt, et il est resté prisonnier en Angleterre de 1415-1440. C'est pendant ces années qu'il a écrit plusieurs de ses poèmes.

~~~~~~~~~~~~

Rondeau

Le temps a **laissé** son manteau
De vent, de froidure[1] et de pluie,
Et s'est **vêtu** de **broderie,**
De soleil luisant[2], clair et beau.

5 Il n'y a bête, ni oiseau,
Qu'en son jargon[3] ne chante ou crie:
Le temps a laissé son manteau!

Rivière, fontaine et **ruisseau**
Portent, en livrée[4] jolie,
10 **Gouttes** d'argent d'orfèvrerie[5],
Chacun s'habille de nouveau:
Le temps a laissé son manteau.

[1] cold   [2] shimmering; glistening
[3] language   [4] uniform
[5] silver crafts; silversmithing

MOTS CLÉS
laisser to leave / leave behind
vêtu(e) dressed
la broderie embroidery
un ruisseau stream
une goutte droplet

À réfléchir...

1. In the poem *Rondeau*, all of the following are indications of spring's arrival *except*: **(Clarify)**

   ☐ sunshine

   ☐ streams fill with fish

   ☐ rivers, fountains, and streams sparkle

   ☐ all of nature looks like new

2. What do the **comptine** *Je te donne pour ta fête* and the poem *Rondeau* have in common? **(Compare and contrast)**

À MARQUER ANALYSE LITTÉRAIRE *Rondeau* is an *allegorical* poem. An *allegory* tells one story that symbolizes something else. What is the poem *Rondeau* an allegory for?

READING TIP A **rondel** or **rondeau** usually has what is called a **rentrement** of the first and second lines of the poem (see "What You Need to Know" on page 138). What line repeats itself in this poem?

READER'S SUCCESS STRATEGY Remember to pay attention to the poem's punctuation. Read *Rondeau* out loud, and let the punctuation tell you where to stop and pause.

~~~~~~~~~~~

Je te donne pour ta fête

Je te donne pour ta fête

Un chapeau de noisette,

Un petit sac en satin

Pour le tenir[6] à la main,

5   Un parasol en soie blanche

Avec des glands[7] sur le manche[8],

Un habit doré[9] sur tranche[10],

Des souliers[11] couleur orange;

Ne les mets que le dimanche

10   Un collier, des bijoux.

      Tiou!

[6] to hold	[7] tassels
[8] handle	[9] golden
[10] seam	[11] shoes

Vocabulaire de la lecture

Mots clés

laisser   *to leave / leave behind*
vêtu(e)   *dressed*
la broderie   *embroidery*
un ruisseau   *stream*
une goutte   *droplet*
un manteau   *coat*

un chapeau   *hat*
un sac   *bag; purse*
la soie   *silk*
un collier   *necklace*
des bijoux   *jewels*

A. Ajoutez le mot clé qui convient le mieux.

1. quelque chose qu'on porte
sur la tête quand il fait froid   _____

2. un tissu de luxe   _____

3. ce qu'on prend pour
porter ses affaires   _____

4. de l'eau qui coule dans les
montagnes, ou dans une forêt   _____

5. on le porte autour du cou   _____

B. Complétez chaque phrase avec le mot clé qui convient le mieux.

1. As-tu vu la femme qui était _____ d'une jolie robe rouge?

2. Je sais qu'il a plu pendant la nuit, parce qu'il y a

des _____ d'eau sur la fenêtre.

3. N'oublie pas ton portefeuille! Tu ne vas pas le _____ ici!

4. Ma grand-mère a de jolis mouchoirs en coton avec

de la _____.

5. Il fait froid dehors. Je vais mettre mon _____.

Tu as compris?

1. Qu'est-ce que le temps a laissé?

_____

2. Maintenant, comment est-ce que le temps s'est vêtu?

_____

3. Que font les bêtes et les oiseaux?

_____

4. En quoi le parasol est-il fait?

_____

5. De quelle couleur sont les souliers?

_____

Connexion personnelle

How would you describe the arrival of spring? Make a list of ideas in the notebook provided.

Le printemps

Avant de lire

Demain, dès l'aube
Chant de nourrice: pour endormir Madeleine

Reading Strategy

DETERMINE THE SUBJECT OF THE POEM Read through the poems several times, at least once out loud. Write down what each poem is about and the words that help you determine the meaning.

DETERMINE THE TONE OF THE POEM How would you characterize the overall tone of the poem? What words contribute to the overall tone of the poems?

DETERMINE THE POEM'S NARRATOR Who is speaking? To whom?

	DEMAIN, DÈS L'AUBE	CHANT DE NOURRICE
Le sujet		
Le ton		
Qui parle?		
À qui?		

What You Need To Know

Both selections, *Demain, dès l'aube* and *Chant de nourrice* are poems written in the first person. *Demain, dès l'aube* was written by Victor Hugo (1802–1855), one of the greatest French Romantic writers. This poem appeared in his collection, *Les Contemplations,* in 1847, just after his daughter and her husband drowned in the Seine.

Chant de nourrice is a song to help a small child go to sleep. It was written by the French poet Marie Noël (1883–1967).

Lectures supplémentaires
Demain, dès l'aube / Chant de
nourrice: pour endormir Madeleine 143

À réfléchir...

1. Look at the underlined section of the poem *Demain, dès l'aube*. What do you think the author means by "les yeux fixé sur mes pensées?" **(Draw Conclusions)**

_____

_____

_____

2. How is the morning described in *Chant de nourrice?* **(Clarify)**

_____

_____

_____

||À MARQUER⟩ **ANALYSE LITTÉRAIRE** Assonance describes the repetition of vowel sounds in neighboring words. Assonance is used in poetry to give the lines a sense of music and continuity. Read the boxed section of *Demain, dès l'aube* and circle all the examples of assonance.

READING TIP In this unit, you've learned to conjugate and use the future tense. As you read both poems, underline all the verbs in the future tense that you come across. Write their infinitives here.

_____

_____

_____

À propos de l'auteur

Victor Hugo est romancier, dramaturge, et poète. Il est peut-être plus connu pour ses romans *Notre-Dame de Paris (The Hunchback of Notre Dame)* (1831) et *Les Misérables* (1862), mais il fut *(was)* d'abord *(first)* poète. Il a commencé à écrire la poésie quand il avait seize ans, et il a publié sa première collection de poèmes quand il avait vingt-cinq ans. Il écrivait dans un style romantique, et il a établi son propre style avec *Notre-Dame de Paris*, son premier roman qui a eu un grand succès.

Demain, dès l'aube

> Demain, dès **l'aube,** à l'heure où blanchit[1]
>   la campagne
> Je partirai. Vois-tu, je sais que tu m'attends.
> J'irai par la forêt, j'irai par la montagne.
> 5 Je ne puis **demeurer** loin de toi plus longtemps.

Je marcherai les yeux fixés[2] sur mes pensées,

Sans rien voir au dehors, sans entendre
        aucun bruit,

Seul, **inconnu,** le dos courbé[3], les mains croisées[4],

10 Triste, et le jour pour moi sera comme la nuit.

Je ne regarderai ni l'or[5] du soir qui tombe,

Ni les **voiles** au loin descendant vers Harfleur,

Et quand j'arriverai, je metterai sur ta tombe

Un bouquet de **houx** vert et de **bruyère** en fleur.

---

[1] whitens   [2] eyes focused on   [3] rounded, curved
[4] crossed   [5] gold

MOTS CLÉS

l'aube dawn
demeurer to live, reside
inconnu(e) unknown

une voile sail (of a sailboat)
le houx holly
la bruyère heather

À propos de l'auteur

Marie Noël est poète et écrivaine. Elle a passé toute sa vie à Auxerre, une petite ville dans la région de Bourgogne. Elle a vécu seule et isolée. Ses poèmes s'inspiraient des chansons du moyen-âge.

~~~~~~~~~~

Chant de nourrice :
pour endormir Madeleine

Dors, mon petit, pour que[6] demain arrive.
Si tu ne dors pas, petite âme vive,
  Demain, le jour le plus gai,
  Demain, ne viendra jamais.

5 Dors, mon petit, pour que les fleurs fleurissent.
Les fleurs qui, la nuit, se parent[7], se lissent[8],
  Si l'enfant reste éveillé,
  N'**oseront** pas s'habiller.

Mais s'il dort, les fleurs en la nuit profonde,
10 N'entendant plus du tout bouger le monde,
  Tout doucement, à tâtons[9],
  Sortiront de leurs boutons[10].

Quand il dormira, toutes les **racines**
Descendront sous terre au fond de[11] leurs mines[12]
15 Chercher pour toutes les fleurs
  Des parfums et des couleurs.

---

[6] so that   [7] adorn themselves; put on their finery
[8] preen themselves   [9] feel one's way   [10] buds
[11] to the depths of   [12] source

MOTS CLÉS
 oser to dare   **une racine** root

Lectures supplémentaires
Demain, dès l'aube / Chant de
nourrice: pour endormir Madeleine **145**

CHALLENGE What do *Demain,
dès l'aube* and *Chant de
nourrice* have in common?
(Compare and contrast)

Les roses alors et les églantines[13],

Vite, fronceront[14] avec leurs épines

   Leurs beaux jupons à volants[15]

20   Rouges, roses, jaunes, blancs.

Les gueules-de-loup[16] et les clématites

Monteront leur coiffe et les marguerites[17]

   Habiles[18] repasseront[19]

   Leur bonnet et leur col[20] rond.

25 Et quand à la fin toutes seront prêtes

En robes de noce[21], en habits de fête,

   Alors, d'un pays lointain

   Arrivera le matin.

---

[13] dog-roses	[14] will gather	[15] flounced petticoats
[16] snapdragons	[17] daisies	[18] clever
[19] will iron	[20] collar	[21] wedding

Vocabulaire de la lecture

Mots clés

l'aube *dawn*

demeurer *to live, reside*

inconnu(e) *unknown*

une voile *sail (of a sailboat)*

le houx *holly*

la bruyère *heather*

oser *to dare*

une racine *root*

un pays *a country*

A. Décidez si les deux mots constituent des antonymes ou des synonymes.

		ANTONYME	SYNONYME
1. oser	hésiter	_____	_____
2. aube	petit matin	_____	_____
3. demeurer	habiter	_____	_____
4. inconnu	familier	_____	_____
5. un pays	une nation	_____	_____

B. Complétez chaque phrase par le mot clé qui convient le mieux.

1. Ah, il fait du vent aujourd'hui. On peut faire de la _____.

2. Souvent, on met du _____ dans la maison pendant la saison de Noël.

3. La _____ est un arbuste *(bush)* violet qu'on trouve surtout en Angleterre.

4. Pour que les plantes poussent bien, il faut arroser *(water)*

leurs _____.

Lectures supplémentaires
Demain, dès l'aube / Chant de
nourrice: pour endormir Madeleine **147**

Tu as compris?

1. Dans le poème *Demain, dès l'aube,* quand il fera jour, qu'est-ce que le narrateur fera?

_____

2. Comment est-ce qu'il marchera?

_____

3. Qu'est-ce qu'il fera quand il arrivera?

_____

4. Dans *Chant de nourrice,* qu'est-ce qui ne viendra pas si l'enfant ne dort pas?

_____

5. Que feront les marguerites pendant la nuit?

_____

Connexion personnelle

Imagine that you are a child responding to the parents from *Chant de nourrice.* What would you say to your parent? Write your ideas in the notebook to the right.

Avant de lire   *Le Pont Mirabeau*

Reading Strategy

DETERMINE THE RHYTHMICAL STRUCTURE OF A POEM Poets use a variety of devices such as repetition, rhyme, and rhythm to create mood and convey meaning. Rhythm, one of the most common poetic devices, is a pattern of stressed and unstressed syllables. When the poem is read aloud, the rhythm can be heard in the greater emphasis on some syllables than on others. Choose four lines of *Le Pont Mirabeau* and write them in the chart below. Indicate the rhythmical pattern that you hear by marking the stressed (') and unstressed (˘) syllables.

_____

_____

_____

_____

What You Need To Know

The pont Mirabeau was built in 1894–1897. A metal bridge that spans the Seine River, it is decorated with four statues representing the city of Paris, and the spirits of Commerce, Navigation, and Abundance. It is said that poet Guillaume Apollinaire (1880–1918) frequently crossed the pont Mirabeau while walking to and from visits with the painter Marie Laurencin, and his home in Auteuil. Apollinaire's relationship with Marie Laurencin ended in 1912, one year prior to the publication of *Le Pont Mirabeau* in *Alcools,* a book that established Apollinaire's reputation as an important poet.

À réfléchir...

1. Which of the following best expresses the main idea of the poem? **(Main Idea)**

☐ Love lasts forever.

☐ Love is best remembered on a bridge.

☐ The happiest memories are those of love.

☐ Time, like the river, passes on, but the painful memories of a love lost remain.

2. How does the two-line refrain enhance the meaning of the poem? **(Draw Conclusions)**

_____

_____

_____

_____

║A MARQUER▷ ANALYSE LITTÉRAIRE You've learned that figurative language is language that means something other than its literal meaning. Read the poem and underline examples of figurative language. Write them here.

_____

_____

_____

READING TIP Sometimes poems do not observe standard writing conventions. Often, for example, each line of a poem starts with a capital letter, even though that line is not the beginning of a new sentence. Poets are free to establish their own style. Note that this poem has no punctuation.

À propos de l'auteur

Guillaume Apollinaire–Wilhelm Apollinaris de Kostrowitsky–est né à Rome d'une mère polonaise et d'un père italien. Il a passé sa jeunesse en France sur la Côte d'Azur, et en 1889, il démenage à Paris où il passera le reste de sa vie sauf deux ans à l'étranger. Il est connu surtout comme poète lyrique mais il est également l'auteur de critiques d'art. Les plus grands sujets de sa poésie sont l'amour, la nostalgie de la jeunesse, et la solitude.

∿∿∿∿∿∿

Le Pont Mirabeau

Sous le pont Mirabeau **coule** la Seine

Et nos amours

Faut-il qu'il m'en **souvienne**

La joie venait toujours après **la peine**

5 Vienne la nuit sonne l'heure

Les jours s'en vont[1] je **demeure**

Les mains dans les mains restons **face à face**

Tandis que sous

Le pont de nos bras passe

10 Des éternels regards l'onde[2] si **lasse**

------

[1] go away   [2] waters

MOTS CLÉS

couler to flow
se souvenir de to remember
la peine sadness, hurt
demeurer to live (on); to stay

face à face face to face
tandis que while
las(se) weary

Vienne la nuit sonne l'heure
Les jours s'en vont je demeure

L'amour s'en va comme cette eau **courante**
L'amour s'en va
15 Comme la vie est lente
Et comme l'**Espérance** est violente

Vienne la nuit sonne l'heure
Les jours s'en vont je demeure

Passent les jours et passent les semaines
20 Ni temps passé
Ni les amours reviennent
Sous le pont Mirabeau coule la Seine

Vienne la nuit sonne l'heure
Les jours s'en vont je demeure

CHALLENGE What do you
think the poet means by the
line "Et comme l'Espérance est
violente"? In what way is hope
violent? **(Make Inferences)**

MOTS CLÉS
courant(e) running

l'espérance hope

Vocabulaire de la lecture

Mots clés

couler *to flow*

se souvenir de *to remember*

la peine *sadness, hurt*

demeurer *to live (on); to stay*

face à face *face to face*

tandis que *while*

las(se) *weary*

courant(e) *running*

l'espérance *hope*

A. Écrivez le mot clé dont le sens est le plus proche du contraire du mot donné.

1. la joie _____

2. énergique _____

3. oublier _____

4. s'en aller _____

5. stagner *(stagnate)* _____

B. Écrivez quatre phrases avec les mots clés qui restent.

1. _____

2. _____

3. _____

4. _____

Tu as compris?

1. Qu'est-ce qui coule sous le pont Mirabeau?

_____

2. Selon le poète, qu'est-ce qui vient toujours après la peine?

_____

3. De quoi est-ce que le poète se souvient?

_____

4. Selon le poète, comment est la vie? Pourquoi?

_____

Connexion personnelle

It happens frequently that looking at one thing reminds us of something else, just as the poet here is reminded of a lost love when he sees the Seine beneath the Pont Mirabeau. Write a short paragraph that describes a memory you have after seeing, listening, smelling, or touching something.

_____
_____
_____
_____
_____
_____
_____
_____
_____
_____
_____

Academic and Informational Reading

In this section you'll find strategies to help you read all kinds of informational materials. The examples here range from magazines you read for fun to textbooks to schedules. Applying these simple and effecive techniques will help you be a successful reader of the many texts you encounter every day.

Reading a Magazine Article

A magazine article is designed to catch and hold your interest. Learning how to recognize the items on a magazine page will help you read even the most complicated articles. Look at the sample magazine article as you read each strategy below.

A Read the **title** and other **headings** to get an idea of what the article is about. The title often presents the article's main topic. Smaller headings may introduce subtopics related to the main topic.

B Note text that is set off in some way, such as an **indented paragraph** or a passage in a **different typeface**. This text often emphasizes an important point or summarizes the article.

C Pay attention to terms within the text in **quotation marks, italics,** or **boldface.** Look for definitions before or after these terms

D Study **visuals**—photos, pictures, charts, or maps. Visuals enrich the text and help bring the topic to life.

||MARK IT UP⟩ Use the sample magazine page on the next page and the tips above to help you answer the following questions.

1. What is this article about? _____

2. Underline the quotation set in italic type that describes the appearance of the baobab.

3. How long can baobabs live?

_____

4. Draw a box around the visual that shows the uses of the baobab tree.

5. According to the visual, what part(s) of the baobab tree are used for medicine?

_____

A # Baobab: The All-Purpose, Topsy-Turvy Tree

Your first reaction on seeing a baobab tree might be to wonder if either it—or you—accidentally were turned upside down. Its fragile branches, which look more like roots, and its unusually thick trunk prompted the famous African explorer, Dr. David Livingstone, to call it "that giant upturned carrot."

B *Dr. David Livingstone called the baobab "that giant upturned carrot."*

D leaves
medicine, condiments

branches
shelter for mammals, reptiles, and insects

bark
cloth, rope, paper, medicine

trunk
nesting for birds, shelter for people

The baobab got its name from Egyptian merchants in the 16th century. Legends about this unusual tree far predate that time, however. According to one legend, it was the gods who overturned the tree to silence its complaints.

Whatever its origin, the baobab definitely looks prehistoric. In fact, many of the baobab trees alive today have been around for over 2,000 years. They can grow to over 60 or more feet tall with a matching diameter. That large girth serves a purpose, though, since the thick, porous bark stores water to sustain the tree during the dry season.

Baobabs produce glowing white blossoms that open at night, but only after the tree is 20 years old. The flowers are short-lived, falling as soon as their nectar is extracted by bats or insects. The fruit is an elongated pod that contains many hard seeds and is called "monkey bread." **C** Monkeys, elephants, and antelope feed on the pods and scatter the seeds in their droppings, ensuring the survival of this one-of-a-kind natural phenomenon.

Reading a Textbook

The first page of a textbook lesson introduces you to a particular topic. The page also provides important information that will guide you through the rest of the lesson. Look at the sample textbook page as you read each strategy below.

A Preview the **title** and other **headings** to find out the lesson's main topic and related subtopics.

B Read the list of **main idea, objectives,** or **focus.** These items summarize the lesson and set the purpose for your reading.

C Look for a list of terms or **vocabulary words.** These words will be identified and defined throughout the lesson.

D Find words set in special type, such as **italics** or **boldface.** Also look for material in parentheses. Boldface is often used to identify the vocabulary terms in a lesson.

E Notice text that is set off in some way on the page, such as in a box. This material may offer **interesting details** or be from a primary source that gives firsthand knowledge or perspective on a topic.

F Examine **visuals,** such as photographs, illustrations, charts, maps, time lines, and their **captions.** Visuals can add information and interest to the topic.

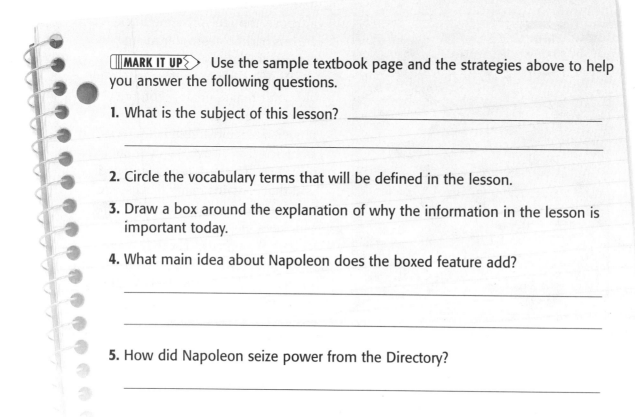

MARK IT UP Use the sample textbook page and the strategies above to help you answer the following questions.

1. What is the subject of this lesson? _____

_____

2. Circle the vocabulary terms that will be defined in the lesson.

3. Draw a box around the explanation of why the information in the lesson is important today.

4. What main idea about Napoleon does the boxed feature add?

_____

_____

5. How did Napoleon seize power from the Directory?

_____

3 Napoleon Forges an Empire [A]

TERMS & NAMES
- Napoleon Bonaparte
- coup d'état [C]
- plebiscite
- lycée
- concordat
- Napoleonic Code
- Battle of Trafalgar

[B] **MAIN IDEA**

A military genius, Napoleon Bonaparte, seized power in France and made himself emperor.

WHY IT MATTERS NOW

In times of political turmoil, military dictators often seize control of nations, as in Haiti in 1991.

SETTING THE STAGE Napoleon was a short man (five feet three inches tall) who cast a long shadow over the history of modern times. He would come to be recognized as one of the world's greatest military geniuses, along with Alexander the Great of Macedonia, Hannibal of Carthage, and Julius Caesar of Rome. In only four years (1795–1799), Napoleon rose from relative obscurity to become master of France.

Napoleon Grasps the Power [A]

[E]

HISTORY MAKERS

**Napoleon Bonaparte
1769–1821**

[F]

Napoleon Bonaparte had a magnetism that attracted the admiration of his men. His speeches were designed to inspire his troops to valorous feats. In one speech, he told soldiers, "If the victory is for a moment uncertain, you shall see your Emperor place himself on the front line."

Bonaparte was generous in his rewards to the troops. Many received the Legion of Honor—a medal for bravery. Sometimes Napoleon would take the medal from his own chest to present it to a soldier. (He kept a few spares in his pocket for these occasions.) A cavalry commander, Auguste de Colbert, wrote, "He awakened in my

Napoleon Bonaparte was born in 1769 on the Mediterranean island [D] of Corsica. When he was nine years old, his parents sent him to a military school in northern France. In 1785, at the age of 16, he finished school and became a lieutenant in the artillery. When the Revolution broke out, Napoleon joined the army of the new government.

Hero of the Hour In October 1795, fate handed the young officer a chance for glory. When royalist rebels marched on the National Convention, a government official told Napoleon to defend the delegates. Napoleon and his gunners greeted the thousands of royalists with a cannonade. Within minutes, the attackers fled in panic and confusion. Napoleon Bonaparte became the hero of the hour and was hailed throughout Paris as the savior of the French republic.

In 1796, the Directory appointed Napoleon to lead a French army against the forces of Austria and the Kingdom of Sardinia. Crossing the Alps, the young general swept into Italy and won a series of remarkable victories, which crushed the Austrian troops' threat to France. Next, in an attempt to protect French trade interests and to disrupt British trade with India, Napoleon led an expedition to Egypt. Unfortunately, his luck did not hold. His army was pinned down in Egypt, and his naval forces were defeated by the British admiral Horatio Nelson. However, he managed to keep the reports of his defeat out of the press, so that by 1799 the words "the general" could mean only one man to the French—Napoleon.

Coup d'État By 1799, the Directory had lost control of the political situation and the confidence of the French people. Only the directors' control of the army kept them in power. Upon Napoleon's return from Egypt, the Abbé Sieyès urged him to seize political power. Napoleon and Josephine, his lovely socialite wife, set a plan in motion. Napoleon met with influential persons to discuss his role in the Directory, while Josephine used her connections with the wealthy directors to influence their decisions. The action began on November 9, 1799, when Napoleon was put in charge of the military. It ended the next day when his troops drove out the members of one chamber of the

Vocabulary [C]
cannonade: a bombardment with heavy artillery fire.

584 Chapter 23

Graphs are used to present information visually. Different kinds of graphs include bar graphs, circle or pie graphs, and line graphs. A *bar graph* compares one or more characteristics of several items. The following tips can help you read a bar graph quickly and accurately. As you read each tip, look at the bar graph on this page.

A Look at the **title** to find out what the graph is about.

B Read the **labels** on the **vertical axis** (up and down) and the **horizontal axis** (side to side) to find out what kind of information is shown.

C Study the **visual pattern** created by the elements in the graph. Which is the tallest? Which is the shortest? What is the relationship between the elements?

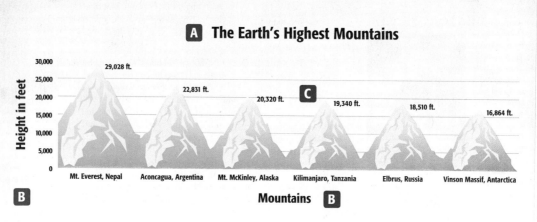

A The Earth's Highest Mountains

Height in feet

30,000
25,000
20,000
15,000
10,000
5,000
0

29,028 ft.   22,831 ft.   20,320 ft.   **C** 19,340 ft.   18,510 ft.   16,864 ft.

Mt. Everest, Nepal   Aconcagua, Argentina   Mt. McKinley, Alaska   Kilimanjaro, Tanzania   Elbrus, Russia   Vinson Massif, Antarctica

B   **Mountains** **B**

|||MARK IT UP⟩ Answer the following questions using the bar graph and the tips above.

1. What is the title of this graph?

_____

2. What information is provided on the vertical axis?

_____

3. Which mountain is located in Africa?

_____

4. How much higher is Mt. Everest than the next highest mountain in the graph?

_____

Reading a Map

To read a map correctly, you have to identify and understand its elements. Look at the example below as you read each strategy in this list.

A Scan the **title** to understand the content of the map.

B Study the **legend,** or **key,** to find out what symbols and colors on the map stand for.

C Look at **geographic labels** to understand specific places on the map.

D Locate the **compass rose,** or **pointer,** to determine direction.

E Check the **scale** to understand how distance is represented on the map.

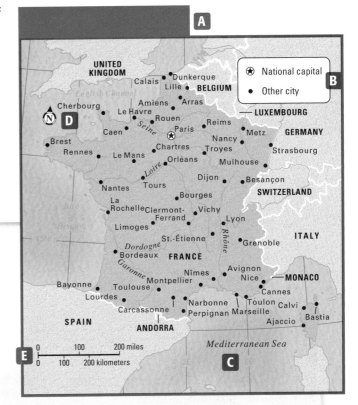

MARK IT UP Use the map to answer the following questions.

1. What is the purpose of this map?

_____

2. What is the capital of France today?

_____

3. Which cities in France lie on the English Channel?

_____

4. About how many kilometers from Marseilles is the island city of Calvi?

_____

Reading a Diagram

Diagrams combine pictures with a few words to provide a lot of information. Look at the example on the opposite page as you read each of the following strategies.

A Look at the **title** to get an idea of what the diagram is about.

B Study the **images** closely to understand each part of the diagram.

C Look at the **captions** and the **labels** for more information.

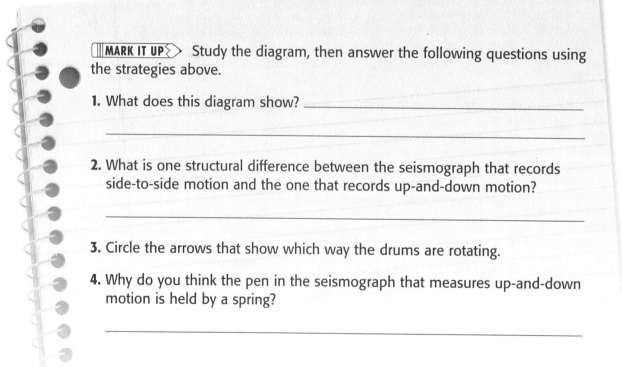

MARK IT UP Study the diagram, then answer the following questions using the strategies above.

1. What does this diagram show? _____

_____

2. What is one structural difference between the seismograph that records side-to-side motion and the one that records up-and-down motion?

_____

3. Circle the arrows that show which way the drums are rotating.

4. Why do you think the pen in the seismograph that measures up-and-down motion is held by a spring?

_____

Seismographs

An instrument called a **seismograph** detects and records waves produced by earthquakes that may have originated hundreds, and even thousands, of kilometers away. Because earthquakes produce different types of wave motions, there are different types of seismographs.

Seismograph A

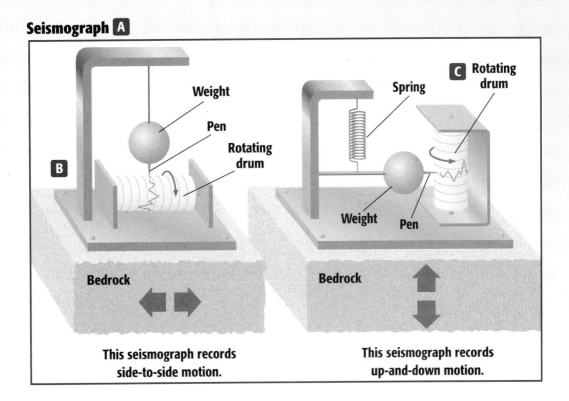

Weight
Pen
Rotating drum
B
Bedrock

This seismograph records side-to-side motion.

C Rotating drum
Spring
Weight
Pen
Bedrock

This seismograph records up-and-down motion.

The *main idea* in a paragraph is its most important point. *Details* in the paragraph support the main idea. Identifying the main idea will help you focus on the central message the writer wants to communicate. Use the following strategies to help you identify a paragraph's main idea and supporting details.

- Look for the **main idea,** which is often the first sentence in a paragraph.

- Use the main idea to help you **summarize** the point of the paragraph.

- Identify specific **details,** including facts and examples, that **support** the main idea.

Moko Jumbies

Main idea

Moko Jumbies are traditional stilt-walking folk characters that were brought to the Caribbean by immigrants from West Africa. Their name comes from a West African god, Moko, and the word *jumbie*, which means "ghost." These "dancing spirits" would prance through the streets on stilts up to 15 feet high wearing long, colorful costumes. To the accompaniment of music—and sometimes, a dwarf in the same costume—they would dance all day, gathering money from onlookers on balconies.

Details

MARK IT UP ＞ Read the following paragraph. Circle the main idea. Then underline the paragraph's supporting details.

Street children on the island of Trinidad have been offered an unusual "leg up" from their poverty-stricken roots. At a training center in the capital city, Port of Spain, they can learn to become Moko Jumbies. There, children as young as four learn to manipulate these tall sticks of wood. As they grow, they graduate to taller stilts, until they can dance ten feet above the streets for 12 hours at a stretch. Rising into the sky, one young Moko jumbie proudly announced he felt "like a little king."

Problem and Solution

Does the proposed solution to a problem make sense? In order to decide, you need to look at each part of the text. Use the following strategies to read the text below.

- Look at the beginning or middle of a paragraph to find the **statement of the problem.**

- Find **details** that explain the problem and tell why it is important.

- Look for the **proposed solution.**

- Identify the **supporting details** for the proposed solution.

- Think about whether the solution is a good one.

A Stoplight Can Prevent Accidents
by Marcel Marcus

Statement of a problem

It happened again last night. Two cars collided at the intersection of West Ave. and Beach St. This is the sixth accident that has taken place at that intersection in the past year. Luckily, no one has been seriously injured or killed so far. But we need to do something before it's too late.

Explanation of problem

This intersection is so dangerous because West Ave. bends around just before the corner of Beach St. This means that drivers or cyclists aren't able to see cars approaching on West Ave. until they're entering the intersection. They have to just take their chances and hope they make it to the other side. Too many don't.

One action that would help eliminate this problem would be to put a stoplight at the intersection. This would allow drivers to proceed safely across in both directions. It would also slow traffic down and force people to pay more attention to their driving. Although it would cost the community some money, think how much it would save in car repairs, personal injuries, and possibly, even lives.

Here's what you can do to help support this solution:
- Stop procrastinating.
- Look at the facts.
- Go to the town hall and sign a petition.

MARK IT UP Use the text and strategies above to answer these questions.

1. Underline the proposed solution.

2. Circle at least one reason that supports this solution.

3. Explain why you think this is or is not a good solution to the problem.

It's important to understand the *sequence*, or order of events, in what you read. This helps you understand what happens and why. The tips below can help you understand sequence in any type of text.

- Read through a passage, looking for the **main steps** or stages.

- Look for **words and phrases that signal time,** such as 1429, May 30, 1431, and the next year.

- Look for **words and phrases that signal order,** such as *meanwhile, finally,* and *after.*

MARK IT UP Read the passage about Joan of Arc on the next page. Then use the information from the article and the tips above to answer the questions.

1. Circle the words or phrases that signal time.

2. Underline the words or phrases that signal order.

3. A time line can help you understand the sequence of events. Use the information from the article to complete this time line.

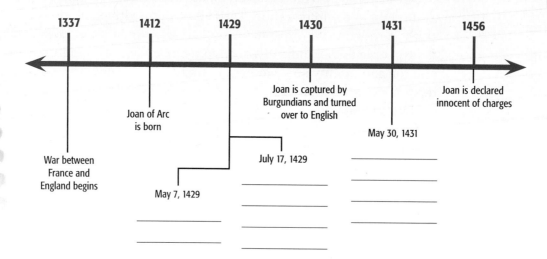

| 1337 | 1412 | 1429 | 1430 | 1431 | 1456 |

War between France and England begins

Joan of Arc is born

May 7, 1429

July 17, 1429

Joan is captured by Burgundians and turned over to English

May 30, 1431

Joan is declared innocent of charges

Joan of Arc

It was 1429. France had been at war with England since 1337. The countries had at last signed a treaty stating that when the French king, Charles VI, died, Henry V of England would become ruler of France.

Meanwhile, in the French countryside, a 17-year-old teenage peasant girl, Joan of Arc, was having visions and hearing voices. She believed these were the saints urging her to help drive the English from France. The voices instructed her to restore the crown to Charles VI's son, her country's true king.

On May 7, 1429, Joan led the French army into battle against an English fort that blocked the roads to the town of Orléans. The English had already been attacking the town for over six months. Without help, the city would be lost, and Joan and her troops needed to take the English fort.

It was a well-matched battle, but the French finally retreated in despair.

Then, without warning, Joan and a few soldiers charged back toward the fort. The entire French army soon followed. They took the fort and ended the siege of Orléans. Joan had helped to turn the tide for France.

After that victory, Joan persuaded Charles to go with her to Reims, where he was crowned king on July 17, 1429. The next year, England's allies, the Burgundians, captured Joan in battle and turned her over to the English. They gave her to authorities of the Church to be put on trial. The English were looking for any excuse to get rid of the teenage girl who had embarrassed them by defeating their army in battle.

Joan of Arc was burned at the stake on May 30, 1431. Charles VII, the king she had risked her life to have crowned, did not come to her aid.

Another trial was held 25 years later, and Joan was declared innocent.

Cause and Effect

A *cause* is an event that brings about another event. An *effect* is something that happens as a result of the first event. Identifying causes and effects helps you understand how events are related. Use the tips below to find causes and effects in any kind of reading.

- Look for an action or event that answers the question, "What happened?" This is the **effect.**

- Look for an action or event that answers the question, "Why did this happen?" This is the **cause.**

- Look for words or phrases that signal causes and effects, such as *because, as a result, therefore, consequently,* and *since.*

MARK IT UP Read the cause-and-effect passage on the next page. Then use the strategies above to help you answer the following questions.

1. Circle words in the passage that signal causes and effects. The first one has been done for you.

2. What two causes are given for cutting down trees in the rain forest?

_____

_____

3. Causes often have multiple effects. Complete the following diagram showing the effects of destruction of the rain forests.

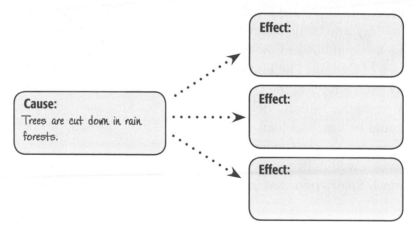

Cause:
Trees are cut down in rain forests.

Effect:

Effect:

Effect:

We're Destroying Our Rain Forests

Imagine a lush, green place that is home to over half of all the animal and plant species on Earth. You don't really have to imagine very hard, because that place—the rain forest—actually exists. The largest rain forest, in the Amazon River basin, covers about 2 million square miles of Brazil, Ecuador, and Peru. Unfortunately, **Effect** rain forests like this one are being destroyed at an increasingly alarming rate.

According to a study done by U.S. and Brazilian scientists, nearly 5 million acres of this rain forest are disappearing a year. That's equal to seven football fields a minute.

The **cause** of this destruction is **Cause** simple—cutting down trees. Every minute, around 2,000 trees are felled to create highways, railroads, and farms. Some trees, such as mahogany and teak, are harvested for their beautiful hardwood.

This destruction of the rain forests has wide-ranging effects. Tens of thousands of plants and animals call the rain forests home—about 30,000 plant species in the Amazon rain forest alone. In addition to important food products such as bananas, coffee, nuts, and chocolate, these plants include medicinal compounds found nowhere else on Earth. As for animals, scientists estimate that an area of just 4 square miles of a rain forest shelters more than 550 species of birds, reptiles, and amphibians. Because their habitat is disappearing, almost 100 species face extinction every day.

Rain forests also act as climate regulators. They balance the exchange of water and carbon dioxide in the atmosphere and help offset global warming. The Earth's well-being will suffer increasingly as a result of the rain forests' destruction.

If this process is not reversed, it may be over within 50 years. The teeming, thriving rain forest will be a thing of the past.

Comparison and Contrast

Comparing two things means showing how they are the same. *Contrasting* two things means showing how they are different. Comparisons and contrasts are often used in science and history books to make a subject clearer. Use these tips to help you understand comparison and contrast in reading assignments such as the article on the opposite page.

- Look for **direct statements** of comparison and contrast. "These things are similar because…" or "One major difference is…"

- Pay attention to **words and phrases that signal comparisons,** such as *also, both, like,* and *in the same way.*

- Notice **words and phrases that signal contrasts.** Some of these are *however, unlike,* and *in contrast.*

MARK IT UP Read the article on the next page. Then use the information from the article and the tips above to answer the questions.

1. Circle the words and phrases that signal comparisons. A sample has been done for you.

2. Underline the words and phrases that signal contrasts. Notice the completed sample.

3. A Venn diagram shows how two subjects are similar and how they are different. Complete this diagram, which uses information from the essay to compare and contrast baguettes and bagels. Add one or more similarity to the center of the diagram and one or more difference to each outer circle.

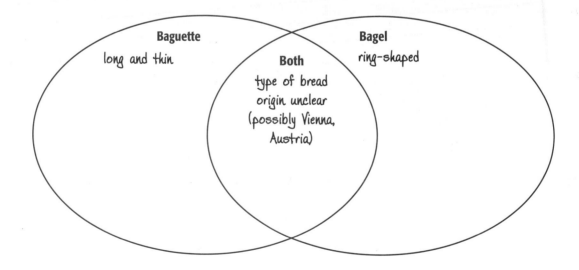

Baguette
long and thin

Both
type of bread
origin unclear
(possibly Vienna,
Austria)

Bagel
ring-shaped

Baguette or Bagel?

Traveling broadens you, as the old saying goes. Part of the reason for this may be that, no matter where you go, you'll find a delicious variety of bread to munch on. Two kinds that you can enjoy today from Paris, France, to Paris, Texas, are the baguette and the bagel.

The origins of both breads are a bit unclear. According to some stories, despite the fact that the baguette has come to symbolize France, it actually was invented in Vienna Austria. A number of historians say the bagel also originated there, but others say it was created in Poland or Russia.

Both baguettes and bagels are made from the same basic ingredients—flour, water, yeast, butter, eggs, sugar, and salt. Different methods are used to prepare them, however. The dough for each bread is similarly mixed, kneaded, and left to rise. Unlike baguettes, though, bagels are boiled in water before they are baked. This process makes them dense and chewy and gives them a very light crust. Baguettes, in contrast, have a soft center surrounded by a crunchy crust.

Another difference between the two types of bread is their shape. The word *baguette* means "wand" or "stick" in French, and that's what the thin, typically two-foot-long baguettes look like. The bagel, on the other hand, is shaped like a ring, and may have been created as a stirrup of dough to honor a Polish king.

Although the standard baguette and bagel are both made from white flour, variations are also available. Baguettes come in sourdough, rye, or whole wheat varieties, or even mixed with a little milk and sugar. In addition to those versions, bagels are available in flavors ranging from apple and blueberry to spinach and tomato.

So the next time you get a craving for bread, try a baguette or a bagel—or forget about choosing, and take both.

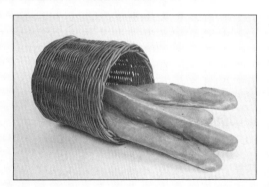

Persuasion is giving an opinion backed up with reasons and facts. Examining an opinion and the reasons and facts that support it will help you decide if the opinion makes sense. Look at the persuasive essay on the next page as you read these tips.

- Look for words or phrases that **signal an opinion,** such as *I believe, I think,* and *in my opinion.*

- Identify reasons, facts, or expert opinions that **support** the writer's position.

- Ask yourself if the writer's position and the reasons that back it up **make sense.**

- Look for **errors in reasoning,** such as overgeneralizations, that may affect the persuasiveness of the writer.

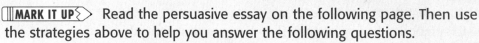 Read the persuasive essay on the following page. Then use the strategies above to help you answer the following questions.

1. Circle any words or phrases that signal an opinion.

2. Underline any words or phrases that signal the writer's opinion.

3. The writer presents both sides of this issue. List the points supporting both sides in the chart below.

Recorders should be allowed	Recorders should not be allowed
Recordings can be an aid to learning.	

THIS SHOULD BE RECORDED

The school board of District 163 just passed a policy banning personal recorders in the schools. I disagree with this decision and believe not only that recorders should be allowed, but also that they can be an aid to learning.

In a public meeting held to discuss this issue, most people supported the policy for two reasons. Some thought that recorders would distract students from their school activities. Others believed that they would tempt students to cut classes. Students would just assign one person to record the lesson and make copies of the recording for everyone else.

In my opinion, neither of these reasons is valid. None of my teachers would ever allow a student to listen to a recording during class. In addition, attendance is a significant part of every student's grade, and most wouldn't risk cutting class, even if someone offered to record it for them. Besides, listening to a recording would take just as long as sitting through the class itself.

More important, though, are the ways recorders can enhance learning.

The first is that recordings can supplement students' notes. Everyone's mind drifts off sometimes, and having a recording of the lesson could help students fill in gaps and clarify confusing points.

The most important role for recorders, however, is in language classes. In other academic areas, students just have to learn specific information. In language classes, however, they also have to remember how words should sound when they're spoken. If students were allowed to record their language lessons, they could use the recording to help improve their speaking skills and supplement the meager hour a week they have in the language lab.

In summary, I think that the policy banning recorders in the schools should be repealed. Students are mature enough to use recording technology to improve, not impede, their academic success. And I believe they should be given the chance.

Social studies class becomes easier when you understand how your textbook's words, pictures, and maps work together to give you information. Following these tips can make you a better reader of social studies lessons. As you read the tips, look at the sample lesson on the right-hand page.

A Read the **headline** and **subheads** of the lesson. These give you an idea what the section covers.

B Make sure you know the meaning of any boldfaced or underlined **vocabulary items.** These terms often appear on tests.

C Think about **how information is organized**. Social studies books often present ideas using sequence, cause and effect, comparison and contrast, and main idea and supporting details.

D Look closely at **graphics** such as maps and illustrations. Think about what information these features add to the text.

E Note items that appear in the **margins of the page**. These often provide questions or additional information that will help you understand and focus your reading.

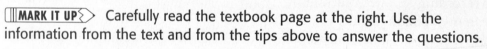**MARK IT UP** Carefully read the textbook page at the right. Use the information from the text and from the tips above to answer the questions.

1. Circle the main idea of this lesson.

2. Underline the sentence that explains an important fact learned from Henry Hudson's voyages.

3. How is the information about Henry Hudson in "One European's Story" presented—by main idea and supporting details, by cause and effect, or by sequence?

_____

4. What information does the map add to the text?

_____

_____

② European Competition in North America

TERMS & NAMES
Henry Hudson
John Cabot
Giovanni da Verrazzano
Jacques Cartier
Spanish Armada
Samuel de Champlain
New France

MAIN IDEA	WHY IT MATTERS NOW
Other European countries competed with Spain for control over territory in the Americas.	European culture has strongly influenced American culture.

ONE EUROPEAN'S STORY

In 1609, an Englishman named <u>Henry Hudson</u> set sail from Europe. He sailed under the Dutch flag and hoped to find a route to China. Arriving at the coast of present-day New York, he sailed up the river that now bears his name. In his journal, Hudson described what he saw.

A VOICE FROM THE PAST

The land is the finest for cultivation that I ever in my life set foot upon, and it also abounds in trees of every description. The natives are a very good people; for, when they saw that I would not remain, they supposed that I was afraid of their bows, and taking the arrows, they broke them in pieces and threw them into the fire.

Henry Hudson, quoted in *Discoverers of America*

Hudson did not find a passage to Asia, but he led another expedition in 1610, this time sailing for the English. He made his way through ice-clogged waters in Canada and entered a large bay, today called Hudson Bay. There he sailed for months, but still found no westward passage.

After enduring a harsh winter, his crew rebelled. They put Hudson, his young son, and several loyal sailors in a small boat and set them adrift (shown at right). Hudson's party was never heard from again.

The Search for the Northwest Passage

Hudson's voyages showed that some European countries hoped to find a westward route to Asia as late as the 1600s. While Spain was taking control of the Americas, other Europeans were sending out expeditions to find the Northwest Passage, a water route through North America to Asia.

One of the first explorers to chart a northern route across the Atlantic in search of Asia was the Italian sailor <u>John Cabot</u>. In 1497, Cabot crossed the Atlantic Ocean to explore for the English. He landed in the area of Newfoundland, Canada. He was certain that he had reached Asia and claimed the land for England. The next year he set sail once

European Exploration of the Americas **67**

Reading a science textbook becomes easier when you understand how the explanations, drawings, and special terms work together. Use the strategies below to help you better understand your science textbook. Look at the examples on the opposite page as you read each strategy in this list.

A Preview the **title** and any **headings** to see what scientific concepts will be covered.

B Read the **key ideas, objectives,** or **focus.** These items summarize the lesson and establish a purpose for your reading.

C Look for **boldfaced** and **italicized** terms that appear in the text. Look for the definitions of these terms.

D Carefully examine any **pictures** or **diagrams.** Read the **captions** and evaluate how the graphics help illustrate and explain the text.

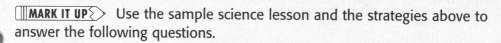 **MARK IT UP** Use the sample science lesson and the strategies above to answer the following questions.

1. What are the two main ideas that will be covered in this lesson?

_____

_____

2. Underline the definition of an ocean current.

3. What direction do ocean currents turn in the Northern Hemisphere?

_____

4. Which other chapter of the book might you need to read to better understand this lesson?

_____

5. Based on the illustration, where do most of the cool currents flow?

_____

24.1

B **KEY IDEAS**

Surface currents are driven primarily by the wind.

There are several types of surface currents.

KEY VOCABULARY

- ocean current
- surface current
- cold-core ring
- warm-core ring
- countercurrent

VISUALIZATIONS
CLASSZONE.COM

Examine global surface currents.
Keycode: ES2401

A Surface Currents

The water in the oceans is constantly on the move. Some motions, such as waves, are obvious. Other types of motion are so subtle or so deep that they are barely noticeable. These movements, called ocean currents, usually involve large water masses. An **ocean current** is any continuous flow of water along a broad path in the ocean. Ocean currents may flow at the surface or far below it.

C A **surface current** is an ocean current that generally flows in the upper 1000 meters of the ocean. Surface currents are primarily driven by the wind. The Global Ocean Currents map below shows surface currents of the world. You can make several observations from the map. First, the Atlantic Ocean and the Pacific Ocean each have two circles of ocean currents, one in the Northern Hemisphere and another in the Southern Hemisphere. Consider as well that the direction in which each current circulates depends on the Coriolis Effect (Chapter 19): hence ocean currents in the Northern Hemisphere turn clockwise, and in the Southern Hemisphere, counterclockwise. As you see, the circular currents of the North Atlantic and North Pacific turn clockwise, while the currents of the South Atlantic and South Pacific turn counterclockwise.

You can also see from this map that the temperature of the currents follows a pattern. Currents flowing away from the equator carry warm water. Currents flowing toward the equator carry cold water. This occurs because areas near the equator have warmer temperatures and areas near the poles have colder temperatures.

D **Global Ocean Currents**

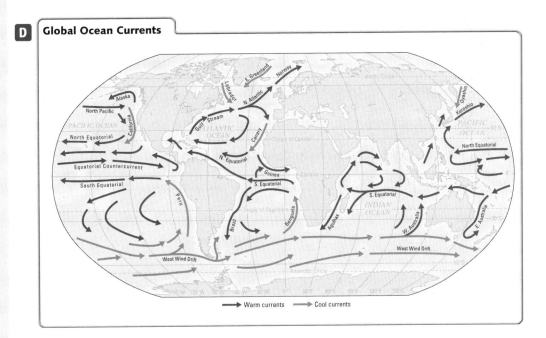

→ Warm currents ⇒ Cool currents

532   **Unit 6** Earth's Oceans

Reading in mathematics is different from reading in history, literature, or science. Use the following strategies to help you better understand your math textbook. Look at the example on the next page as you read each strategy.

A Preview the **title** and **headings** to see which math concepts will be covered or reviewed.

B Find and read the **goals** or **instructions** for completing the lesson. These will tell you the most important points to know and how to proceed.

C Identify **vocabulary** and **concepts** you will be responsible for understanding and applying.

D Study any **worked-out solutions** to sample problems. These are the key to understanding how to complete the exercises.

|||MARK IT UP▷ Use the strategies above and the mathematics lesson on the next page to answer the following questions.

1. What is the purpose of this lesson? _____

_____

2. Circle the instructions for completing the lesson.

3. Underline the vocabulary terms you will need to define.

4. How many exercises do you have to complete in item 9.5?

_____

5. This lesson lists a page where you can find the definition of a tangent and later gives the definition itself. Put a box around each.

LESSONS 9.5 TO 9.6

Notebook Review A

Check Your Definitions

trigonometric ratio, p. 463   cosine, p. 463

sine, p. 463   tangent, p. 463

C

Use Your Vocabulary

1. Copy and complete: To write the sine ratio for a given acute angle of a right triangle, you need to know the length of the side ? the angle and the length of the ? .

9.5 Can you find side lengths of special right triangles?

 EXAMPLE Find the length of the hypotenuse. Give the exact answer.

hypotenuse = leg · $\sqrt{2}$ Rule for 45°-45°-90° triangle

= $26\sqrt{2}$ Substitute.

ANSWER The length of the hypotenuse is $26\sqrt{2}$ feet.

✓ **Find the value of each variable. Give the exact answer.**

2.   **3.**    **4.**

9.6 Can you use trigonometric ratios?

 EXAMPLE In △ABC, write the sine, cosine, and tangent ratios for ∠A. **D**

$\sin A = \dfrac{\text{opposite}}{\text{hypotenuse}} = \dfrac{12}{37}$

$\cos A = \dfrac{\text{adjacent}}{\text{hypotenuse}} = \dfrac{35}{37}$

$\tan A = \dfrac{\text{opposite}}{\text{adjacent}} = \dfrac{12}{35}$

Reading an Application

Reading and understanding an application will help you fill it out correctly and avoid mistakes. Use the following strategies to understand any application. Refer to the example on the next page as you read each strategy.

A **Begin at the top.** Scan the application to understand the different sections.

B Look for special **warnings, conditions,** or **instructions for filling out** the application.

C Note any **references** that must be included with the application.

D Pay attention to **optional sections,** or **questions you don't have to answer.**

E Look for **difficult or confusing words** or abbreviations. Look them up in a dictionary or ask someone what they mean.

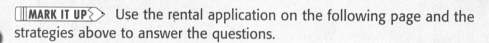 Use the rental application on the following page and the strategies above to answer the questions.

1. Circle the part of the application that asks about your bank accounts.

2. What information do you have to supply about your current job besides name, address, and phone number of your employer?

   _____

3. When is rent due?

   _____

4. Who would be responsible for the damage caused if your bathtub overflowed?

   _____

5. **ASSESSMENT PRACTICE** Circle the letter of the correct answer.
   If you are renting an apartment with a roommate, your roommate should
   A. sign the bottom of your application next to your name.
   B. fill out a separate application.
   C. complete the information for Personal Reference.
   D. make a copy of your application and sign it.

A Apartment Rental Application

NAME OF APPLICANT   HOME PHONE NUMBER   DATE

PRESENT ADDRESS

PRESENT LANDLORD   ADDRESS   PHONE NUMBER

CURRENT EMPLOYER   ADDRESS   PHONE NUMBER

POSITION   TYPE OF BUSINESS   SALARY   LENGTH OF EMPLOYMENT

PERSONAL REFERENCE (NAME) **C** ADDRESS   PHONE NUMBER

EMERGENCY CONTACT (NAME)   ADDRESS   PHONE NUMBER

BANK-CHECKING ACCOUNT   ACCOUNT NUMBER

BANK-SAVINGS ACCOUNT   ACCOUNT NUMBER

NAMES OF ALL CO-TENANTS (EACH ADULT MUST COMPLETE A SEPARATE APPLICATION) **D**

APARTMENT NO./TYPE   TOTAL NO. OF OCCUPANTS   RENT PER MONTH $

ADDRESS

LEASE TERM (MONTHS)   FROM (DATE)   TO (DATE)

Rent is due on the first day of each month in advance.
The applicant authorizes the renting agency to obtain a consumer credit report for the applicant. **B**
The owner and the management are not responsible for the loss of personal belongings caused by fire, theft, smoke, water or otherwise, unless caused by their negligence. **E**

Signature_____

Reading a Public Notice

Public notices can tell you about events in your community and give you valuable information about safety. When you read a public notice, follow these tips. Each tip relates to a specific part of the notice on the next page.

A Read the notice's **title,** if it has one. The title often gives the main idea or purpose of the notice.

B Pay attention to information presented in **different typefaces,** such as boldface or underline. This often indicates main topics or subtopics.

C Look for **details** about where and when events will take place.

D Look for **descriptions** of individual events.

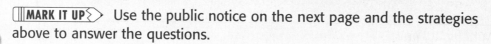 Use the public notice on the next page and the strategies above to answer the questions.

1. What is the purpose of this notice?

_____

2. Circle the date and time of the meeting of the Committee to Restore George Washington's Portrait.

3. Put a star next to the meetings that will NOT be held at the Town Hall.

4. If you are interested in the proposed smoking ban, what meeting should you attend?

_____

5. ASSESSMENT PRACTICE Circle the letter of the correct answer.
When will permits for house additions be discussed?
A. Thursday, August 7, 7:00 P.M.
B. Monday, August 11, 7:00 P.M.
C. Wednesday, August 20, 4:00 P.M.
D. Thursday, August 21, 7:00 P.M.

Meetings ⒶA

Planning Board:
    Tuesday, Aug. 5, 7 P.M., Town Hall.
Committee to Restore George Washington's Portrait: ⒷB
    Wednesday, Aug. 6, 5 P.M., Town Hall.
Grant Committee:
    Wednesday, Aug. 6, 7 P.M., Town Hall. ⒸC
Conservation Commission:
    Thursday, Aug. 7, 7 P.M., Town Hall.
    Agenda (specific times for individual hearings not given):
    <u>Public Hearing</u> concerning a Request for Amendment to the Order of
    Conditions issued to the Department of Public Works for sewer and storm
    drain replacement;
    ⒷB <u>Public Hearing</u> concerning a Request for Determination for a proposed
    roof to be installed over an existing open deck;
    ⒹD <u>Public Hearing</u> concerning a Stormwater Permit Application in conjunction
    with construction of a two-story addition on Adams Street;
    <u>Public Hearing</u> concerning a Stormwater Permit Application in conjunction
    with construction of a two-story addition on Kimball Road.
Board of Health:
    Monday, Aug. 11, 6 P.M., Town Hall. Agenda: Consideration of and vote on
    proposed smoking ban.
Building, Planning, and Construction Committee:
    Monday, Aug. 11, 7 P.M., Endicott Estate.
Finance Committee:
    Thursday, Aug. 14, 7 P.M., Town Hall.
Board of Assessors:
    Wednesday, Aug. 20, 4 P.M., Town Hall.
School Committee:
    Wednesday, Aug. 20, 7 P.M., School Administration Building.
Board of Selectmen:
    Thursday, Aug. 21, 7 P.M., Town Hall.
Conservation Commission:
    Thursday, Aug. 21, 7 P.M., Town Hall.
Library Trustees:
    Tuesday, Aug. 26, 7 P.M., Endicott Branch Library.

Reading a Web Page

When you research information for a report or project, you may use the World Wide Web. Once you find the site you want, the strategies below will help you find the facts and details you need. Look at the sample Web page on the right as you read each of the strategies.

A Notice the page's **Web address,** or URL. You may want to write it down or bookmark it if you think you might access the page at another time.

B Look for **menu bars** along the top, bottom, or side of the page. These guide you to other parts of the site that may be useful.

C Look for **links** to other parts of the site or to related pages. Links are often highlighted in color or underlined.

D Use a search **feature** to quickly find out whether the information you want to locate appears anywhere on the site.

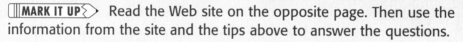 Read the Web site on the opposite page. Then use the information from the site and the tips above to answer the questions.

1. Circle the Web address of this site.

2. Which menu option would you click to view comments from other visitors to the site?

_____

3. Put a star by the link that includes information about job openings for Creole speakers.

4. Draw a box around the links you would click to get information about the Crisis in Education.

5. ASSESSMENT PRACTICE Circle the letter of the correct answer.
   What is Learning Crisis?

   A. a chatroom

   B. a Web page for teachers

   C. a feature article

   D. the English translation of a Creole Web site

Back **Forward** **Reload** **Home** **Images** **Print** **Security** **Stop** L

Location: http://www.creolelink.com/edu&/index.html A

B | **Search** | **Chat** | **Check E-mails** | **Message Boards** | **Subscribe** | **Site Map**

Creole Link

Links C

Fine Arts
Entertainment
Politics
Lifestyle
Finance
Careers
Technology
Education
Resources
Sports

Education

Crisis in Education

Part I
Part II
Part III
Part IV

Features

Dr. François Lescay, Math Professor Extraordinaire

Learning Crisis

First Creole-Language Virtual University in U.S.

D Web Site Search

Reading Technical Directions

Reading technical directions will help you understand how to use the products you buy. Use the following tips to help you read a variety of technical directions.

A Look carefully at any **diagrams** or **other images** of the product.

B **Read all the directions** carefully at least once before using the product.

C Notice **headings** or **lines** that separate one section from another.

D Look for **numbers** or **letters** that give the steps in sequence.

E Watch for **warnings** or **notes** with more information.

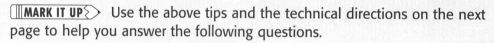 Use the above tips and the technical directions on the next page to help you answer the following questions.

1. What uses of a cordless phone do these technical directions explain?

   _____

2. Circle the headings that describe two ways you can make calls with this phone.

3. What should you do if you have a noisy connection?

   _____

4. Draw a box around the step that is the same whether you're making calls with the handset or with the base unit.

5. **ASSESSMENT PRACTICE** Circle the letter of the correct answer.
   These directions do NOT tell you how to

   A. switch a call with the handset to the speakerphone.

   B. hang up using the handset and the base unit.

   C. answer a call with the handset off the base unit.

   D. make a call using the speed dial feature.

Using a Cordless Phone

Making Calls

With the Handset

B 1 Press (TALK ON/OFF).

2 Dial a phone number.

3 To hang up, press (TALK ON/OFF) or put the handset on the base unit.

- If noise is interfering with your conversation, press (CH) to choose a clearer channel or move closer to the base unit.

- To switch a call to the speakerphone, press (REMOTE SP). To hang up, press (SP-PHONE) or (REMOTE SP).

- Like a standard phone, you can dial with the base unit keypad after pressing (TALK ON/OFF).

With the Base Unit

D 1 Press (SP-PHONE).

2 Dial a phone number.

3 Speak into the (MIC). To hang up, press (SP-PHONE).

A

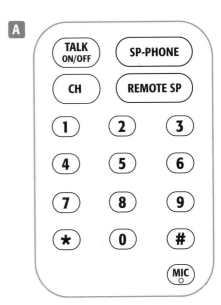

Answering Calls **C**

With the Handset

If the handset is off the base unit, press (TALK ON/OFF). OR If the handset is on the base unit, just lift up.

With the Base Unit

Press (SP-PHONE), then speak into the (MIC).

- If the handset is off the base unit, you can also answer the call by pressing any dial button (0 to 9, *****, or #). **E**

Reading Product Information: Safety Guidelines

Safety guidelines are facts and recommendations provided by government agencies or product manufacturers offering instructions and warnings about safe use of their products. Learning to read and follow such guidelines is important for your safety. Look at the sample guidelines as you read each strategy below.

A Read the **title** to find out what the safety guidelines focus on.

B Read the **recommendations** that product owners and users should follow to ensure safe usage of the product.

C Pay close attention to the **hazards** associated with the product.

D Look for **contact information** that tells you where to call or write to report dangerous products or product-related injuries.

A SAFEGUARDS FOR USING YOUR FOOD PROCESSOR

When using electrical appliances, these basic safety precautions should always be followed:

- Read all instructions carefully before use. **B**
- To protect against electric shock, do not put the base of the appliance in water or any other liquid.
- Close supervision is necessary when the appliance is used by or near children.
- Unplug from the outlet when not in use, before putting on or taking off parts, and before cleaning.
- Avoid contact with moving parts of the appliance.
- Do not operate any appliance with a damaged cord or plug or after the appliance malfunctions, or is dropped or damaged in any manner. Return the appliance to nearest authorized Consumer Service Center for examination, repair, or adjustment. **C**
- The use of attachments not recommended or sold by the manufacturer may cause fire, electric shock, or injury.
- Do not use the appliance outdoors.
- Do not let the cord hang over the edge of a table or counter, or touch hot surfaces.

To report a defective or dangerous product, call (800) 555-5377. D

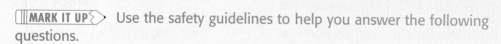 **MARK IT UP** Use the safety guidelines to help you answer the following questions.

1. Underline the precaution you should take when the food processor is running.

2. What should you do with a damaged appliance?

_____

3. Put a box around the step to take before cleaning the food processor.

4. ASSESSMENT PRACTICE Circle the letter of the correct answer.
In which situation can the food processor be safely operated?
   A. outdoors
   B. using recommended attachments
   C. in the sink
   D. on a hot stove

Reading a Museum Schedule

Knowing how to read a museum schedule accurately can help you plan your visit. Look at the example as you read each strategy on this list.

A Look at the **title** to know what the schedule covers.

B Identify **labels** that show dates or **days of the week** to help you understand how the daily or weekly schedule works.

C Look for **expressions of time** to know what hours or minutes are listed on the schedule.

D Look for **changes** or **exceptions** to the regular schedule.

A Museum of Science and Industry
Summer Hours (June 14–Labor Day)

Daily: 9:30 A.M.–7:00 P.M. **C**

Discovery Space: 9:30 A.M.–6:00 P.M.
(special area for children 6 and under)

Notes: Hands-on Labs are usually open from 10:00 A.M.–5:30 P.M. during the summer. These hours, however, are subject to change. Call ahead. **D**

Submarine Summer Tour Hours

Regular Tour   Daily: 10:00 A.M.–5:30 P.M. $5.00

Tech Tour **B** First Sunday of each month $15.00 (Call for schedule)

Please note that you must be at least 3 years old to tour the sub. **D**

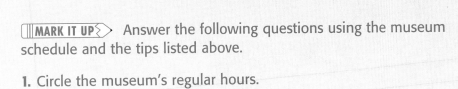 **MARK IT UP** Answer the following questions using the museum schedule and the tips listed above.

1. Circle the museum's regular hours.

2. Who is not allowed to tour the submarine?

_____

3. When does the Discovery Space close?

_____

4. **ASSESSMENT PRACTICE** Circle the letter of the correct answer.
   What should you do if you want to visit the Hands-on Labs?
   A. Plan to go on the first Sunday of the month.
   B. Bring a child over the age of six with you.
   C. Check to see what hours it is open.
   D. Make arrangements by calling 503-555-4624.

Test Preparation Strategies

In this section you'll find strategies and practice to help you with many different kinds of standardized tests. The strategies apply to questions based on long and short readings, as well as questions about charts, graphs, and product labels. You'll also find examples and practice for revising-and-editing tests and writing tests. Applying the strategies to the practice materials and thinking through the answers will help you succeed in many formal testing situations.

Test Preparation Strategies

You can prepare for tests in several ways. First, study and understand the content that will be on the test. Second, learn as many test-taking techniques as you can. These techniques will help you better understand the questions and how to answer them. Following are some general suggestions for preparing for and taking tests. Starting on page 000, you'll find more detailed suggestions and test-taking practice.

Successful Test Taking

 Study Content Throughout the Year

1. **Master the content of your class.** The best way to study for tests is to read, understand, and review the content of your class. Read your daily assignments carefully. Study the notes that you have taken in class. Participate in class discussions. Work with classmates in small groups to help one another learn. You might trade writing assignments and comment on your classmates' work.

2. **Use your textbook for practice.** Your textbook includes many different types of questions. Some may ask you to talk about a story you just read. Others may ask you to figure out what's wrong with a sentence or how to make a paragraph sound better. Try answering these questions out loud and in writing. This type of practice can make taking a test much easier.

3. **Learn how to understand the information in charts, maps, and graphic organizers.** One type of test question may ask you to look at a graphic organizer, such as a spider map, and explain something about the information you see there. Another type of question may ask you to look at a map to find a particular place. You'll find charts, maps, and graphic organizers to study in your textbook. You'll also find charts, maps, and graphs in your science, mathematics, literature, and social studies textbooks. When you look at these, ask yourself, What information is being presented and why is it important?

4. **Practice taking tests.** Use copies of tests you have taken in the past or in other classes for practice. Every test has a time limit, so set a timer for 15 or 20 minutes and then begin your practice. Try to finish the test in the time you've given yourself.

☑ Reading Check In what practical way can your textbook help you prepare for a test?

5. Talk about test-taking experiences. After you've taken a classroom test or quiz, talk about it with your teacher and classmates. Which types of questions were the hardest to understand? What made them difficult? Which questions seemed easiest, and why? When you share test-taking techniques with your classmates, everyone can become a successful test taker.

Use Strategies During the Test

1. Read the directions carefully. You can't be a successful test taker unless you know exactly what you are expected to do. Look for key words and phrases, such as *circle the best answer, write a paragraph,* or *choose the word that best completes each sentence.*

2. Learn how to read test questions. Test questions can sometimes be difficult to figure out. They may include unfamiliar language or be written in an unfamiliar way. Try rephrasing the question in a simpler way using words you understand. Always ask yourself, What type of information does this question want me to provide?

3. Pay special attention when using a separate answer sheet. If you accidentally skip a line on an answer sheet, all the rest of your answers may be wrong! Try one or more of the following techniques:

- Use a ruler on the answer sheet to make sure you are placing your answers on the correct line.

- After every five answers, check to make sure you're on the right line.

- Each time you turn a page of the test booklet, check to make sure the number of the question is the same as the number of the answer line on the answer sheet.

- If the answer sheet has circles, fill them in neatly. A stray pencil mark might cause the scoring machine to count the answer as incorrect.

4. If you're not sure of the answer, make your best guess. Unless you've been told that there is a penalty for guessing, choose the answer that you think is likeliest to be correct.

5. Keep track of the time. Answering all the questions on a test usually results in a better score. That's why finishing the test is important. Keep track of the time you have left. At the beginning of the test, figure out how many questions you will have to answer by the halfway point in order to finish in the time given.

☑ **Reading Check** What are at least two good ways to avoid skipping lines on an answer sheet?

Understand Types of Test Questions

Most tests include two types of questions: multiple choice and open-ended. Specific strategies will help you understand and correctly answer each type of question.

A **multiple-choice question** has two parts. The first part is the question itself, called the stem. The second part is a series of possible answers. Usually four possible answers are provided, and only one of them is correct. Your task is to choose the correct answer. Here are some strategies to help you do just that.

1. Read and think about each question carefully before looking at the possible answers.

2. Pay close attention to key words in the question. For example, look for the word *not*, as in "Which of the following is not a cause of the conflict in this story?"

3. Read and think about all of the possible answers before making your choice.

4. Reduce the number of choices by eliminating any answers you know are incorrect. Then, think about why some of the remaining choices might also be incorrect.

   • If two of the choices are pretty much the same, both are probably wrong.

   • Answers that contain any of the following words are usually incorrect: *always, never, none, all,* and *only.*

5. If you're still unsure about an answer, see if any of the following applies:

   • When one choice is longer and more detailed than the others, it is often the correct answer.

   • When a choice repeats a word that is in the question, it may be the correct answer.

   • When two choices are direct opposites, one of them is likely the correct answer.

   • When one choice includes one or more of the other choices, it is often the correct answer.

   • When a choice includes the word *some* or *often*, it may be the correct answer.

   • If one of the choices is *All of the above*, make sure that at least two of the other choices seem correct.

   • If one of the choices is *None of the above*, make sure that none of the other choices seems correct.

An **open-ended test item** can take many forms. It might ask you

☑ **Reading Check** What words in a multiple-choice question probably signal a wrong answer?

to write a word or phrase to complete a sentence. You might be asked to create a chart, draw a map, or fill in a graphic organizer. Sometimes, you will be asked to write one or more paragraphs in response to a writing prompt. Use the following strategies when reading and answering open-ended items:

1. If the item includes directions, read them carefully. Take note of any steps required.

2. Look for key words and phrases in the item as you plan how you will respond. Does the item ask you to identify a cause-and-effect relationship or to compare and contrast two or more things? Are you supposed to provide a sequence of events or make a generalization? Does the item ask you to write an essay in which you state your point of view and then try to persuade others that your view is correct?

3. If you're going to be writing a paragraph or more, plan your answer. Jot down notes and a brief outline of what you want to say before you begin writing.

4. Focus your answer. Don't include everything you can think of, but be sure to include everything the item asks for.

5. If you're creating a chart or drawing a map, make sure your work is as clear as possible.

☑ **Reading Check** What are at least three key strategies for answering an open-ended question?

DIRECTIONS Following is a selection titled, "Toussaint L'Ouverture." Read the passage carefully. The notes in the side columns will help you prepare for the types of questions that are likely to follow a reading like this. You might want to preview the questions on pages 200–201 before you begin reading.

Toussaint L'Ouverture

In the mid-1700s, on the French-occupied island of Saint-Domingue (now Haiti), François-Dominique Toussaint was born. His father was the son of an African king. Toussaint would become the liberator of his country.

Revolt Toussaint was a hard worker and commanded great respect. In 1791, he joined a revolt against the French occupiers of Saint-Domingue. Many plantations were destroyed, and the insurrection was operating without a clear plan. Toussaint put together an army of his own and trained his men in guerilla tactics. The soldiers called him L'Ouverture—French for "opening"—because of his skill in finding and making openings in enemy lines. From then on, he was known as Toussaint L'Ouverture.

Toussaint was a clever diplomat as well as military leader, and was able to get the better of almost anyone who stood in his way. After France and Spain went to war in 1793, Toussaint joined the Spanish army in Santo

NOTES

READING STRATEGIES FOR ASSESSMENT

Identify the main idea of the article. The title and first paragraph tell you what the author wants to focus on.

196   Lectures pour tous

Discovering French, Nouveau! Level 2

Domingo—the eastern part of Hispaniola, the large island which included Saint-Domingue. His military victories there helped to bring the French army to the brink of disaster.

Social and Political Changes The next year, however, France freed the slaves, and Toussaint rejoined the French army. Although he received much criticism for his turnabout, the move showed his devotion to his people's freedom. Toussaint was instrumental in restoring the economy and easing racial tensions. Many planters who had fled the country were welcomed back, and the former slaves received much better treatment as freed laborers. They received a share of the plantations' profits.

Toussaint's renewed alliance with France also had far-reaching political and military consequences. He was named lieutenant governor of Saint-Domingue and brought his power to bear against his former allies, Spain and Britain. He ousted the Spanish forces from the island and inflicted damaging losses on the British.

His political and military accomplishments continued. Toussaint was promoted to governor-general in 1796. In three years, he forced the British to completely withdraw from the country. Saint-Domingue soon became

Make inferences. Why do you think Toussaint decided to fight with Spain against France?

Note supporting details. What actions did Toussaint take to help bolster the economy of Saint-Domingue?

a trading partner with its former occupiers. Toussaint also sold sugar to the United States and promised not to invade it, receiving arms and manufactured goods in return.

Clarify cause-and-effect relationships. Read carefully to determine Toussaint's motivations. Why did he side with the United States in its war with France?

In 1798, war broke out between the United States and France. Always keeping his people's welfare foremost, Toussaint agreed to oppose the French in return for U.S. military and economic aid.

Emancipation A year after that naval war ended, he sent his army into Santo Domingo, which was still under the control of Spain. He freed the slaves and took control of the entire island of Hispaniola. Glorying in his victory, Toussaint named himself governor-general of the whole island for life. Unfortunately, his life would not last long.

Since France, the United States, and Britain were finally at peace, Napoleon Bonaparte tried to regain control of Hispaniola. He invaded the island and succeeded in defeating Toussaint's forces. In May 1802, Toussaint surrendered, but only on the condition that slavery would not be restored. He was taken to France, where he died in a dungeon less than a year later.

Draw conclusions. What does this action tell you about Toussaint's devotion to his people and their cause?

Toussaint's general, Jean-Jacques Dessalines, took up the fight for freedom where Toussaint had left off. He drove out Napoleon's forces and,

Focus on topic sentences. Look for details that explain how Dessalines continued the fight for freedom.

on January 1, 1804, declared Saint-Domingue an independent country. He called the country Haiti, which means "mountainous land" in the language of the native Arawak inhabitants of the island. Toussaint's dream had become a reality.

Now answer questions 1–6. Base your answers on the selection "Toussaint L'Ouverture." Then check yourself by reading through the Answer Strategies in the side columns.

ANSWER STRATEGIES

Review what *purpose* means. An author's purpose is the main reason he or she is writing. Don't forget that an article that is intended to inform readers can also be entertaining and persuasive.

1 What is the author's purpose in this selection?

    A. to persuade readers to fight all forms of slavery

    B. to compare Toussaint with Napoleon Bonaparte

    C. to entertain readers with an exciting story of triumph over adversity

    D. to describe the accomplishments of a remarkable man

Remember the order of events. One of the choices happened after Toussaint joined the rebellion. One never happened at all. Skim the selection to refresh your memory.

2 What did Toussaint do during the rebellion?

    A. He forged an alliance with Spain.

    B. He made sure his family was safe.

    C. He formed a guerilla army.

    D. He worked hard and commanded respect.

Think about the material. This question asks you to make an inference from what you read. Consider what mattered most to Toussaint. What would have caused him to switch sides?

3 Why might Toussaint have chosen to fight against France in its war with Spain?

    A. Spain offered him a high military position.

    B. France would not allow him to practice guerilla warfare.

    C. France supported slavery in Saint-Domingue.

    D. Spain promised to free all the slaves on Hispaniola.

4 Which of the following was NOT a direct result of Toussaint's renewing his alliance with France?

   A. trade relationships with the United States and Britain

   B. economic growth

   C. better treatment for the former slaves

   D. expulsion of Spain and weakening of Britain in Hispaniola

> **Pay attention to key words.** The key word in this question is *not*. Three of the answers were results of Toussaint's siding with France. Choose the one that happened later and for other reasons.

5 Which statement is true of Haiti?

   A. It was named after Toussaint's royal African grandfather.

   B. It consists of the former colonies of Saint-Domingue and Santo Domingo.

   C. Its name means "mountainous land" in the Arawak language.

   D. It has a statue of Toussaint L'Ouverture at the mouth of Port-au-Prince harbor.

> **Skim the selection.** All the answers sound plausible, but two are not mentioned in the selection and one is an incorrect interpretation. Reread the article to eliminate those and locate the correct answer.

6 In what ways did Toussaint show his commitment to his people?

> **Plan your response.** Reread the selection, looking for actions that showed Toussaint's commitment to his people. Notice how the writer presents and explains relevant details in chronological order

Sample short response for question 6:

Toussaint did all he could to free his people. First, he joined their rebellion. When he saw it wasn't effective, he formed his own army. He then fought with Spain against the French, but supported France when it freed the slaves. He improved both racial relations and the country's economy, and again turned against France to get U.S. aid for his people. He surrendered to France and died a martyr, but only after making sure that slavery itself was dead.

Reading Test Practice
LONG SELECTIONS

DIRECTIONS Now it's time to practice what you've learned about reading test items and choosing the best answers. Read the following selection, "Quebec: Je me souviens." Use the side columns to make notes as you read the passage, focusing on: important ideas, comparisons and contrasts, causes and effects, difficult vocabulary, interesting details, questions you have, predictions you make, and conclusions you draw.

Quebec: *Je me souviens*

According to the well-known saying, all roads lead to Rome, not to Quebec. Many rivers run through Quebec, though, and its Algonquin Indian name means "where the river narrows." It is also the oldest and largest of the Canadian provinces—and a unique crossroads of geography, cultures, languages, and people.

French Colony For 75 years after Canada was first colonized by the French in 1534, the only visitors to Quebec were fishermen and fur traders. Samuel de Champlain founded the city of Quebec in 1608. By 1642, Montreal had been established to the west on the St. Lawrence River. Beyond that was Iroquois country. Daring settlers did push on, though, setting up some outposts as far away as present-day Pittsburgh.

For more than 100 years, the British fought the French for possession of the new land. In 1763, Great Britain took over control of Canada. Eleven years later, the Quebec Act was passed, upholding French civil law and freedom of worship. Canada was then divided and reunited, and Quebec was renamed Lower Canada and then Canada East. Finally, in 1867, Canada became a confederation, and Quebec took back its rightful name.

Province or Nation? In the 1960s, activists in the province began demanding that Quebec also take back its rightful language and culture and become a separate French-speaking nation. That didn't happen; but, in 1969, parents were given the legal right to send their children to either French- or English-speaking schools. Five years later, French became the official language of Quebec.

Since that time, the issue of Quebec's independence—or separatism—has been batted back and forth in the courts and polling booths. In 1995, the Parti Québécois was elected and put Quebec's independence to a vote. The bill was defeated by a small margin and the party was voted out of office in 2003. Quebec has given Canada four of its prime ministers, but the struggle for the province's political identity continues.

Geography and Climate With an area of about 595,000 square miles, Quebec dwarfs France. Stretching over 1,200 miles from north to south, it can comfortably hold the state of Alaska or two of Texas. It includes 15.4% of Canada's total land area.

Quebec is rich in water, too, boasting the 2,100-mile St. Lawrence–Great Lakes system. This system drains about a third of Quebec. Another watershed system covers over 350,000 square miles and flows westward into James and Hudson bays. The St. Lawrence Seaway connects the United States and Canada and is a shipping route used by cargo vessels from around the world. It is an important source of hydroelectric power, and most of Quebec's people and industry are located along it.

Because Quebec covers such a large area, its climate varies greatly depending on the location. It has recorded temperature extremes from 104° F to -65.9° F. While the southern parts of the province don't usually go much below 10° F or above 70° F, temperatures in the far north average -10° F in the winter and only about 49° F in the summer.

The south gets an average of about 41 inches of rain and 87 inches of snow a year, compared with about 18 inches of rain and almost 81 inches of snow in the north. So residents or visitors who want a relatively warm climate have to take it relatively wet as well.

People British settlers had been joining the French in Quebec since 1763. By the middle of the 19th century its population consisted of just under 80% French, about 20% British, and the rest a mix of native peoples and other ethnic groups. The percentage of French people stayed about the same until 1970, when it began increasing slightly. In contrast, more than half the British population has been replaced by people of other ethnic groups. Until the 1970s, most of these immigrants were

European. Since then—as in the rest of North America—almost 70% have come from Asia, the Caribbean, and Latin America.

In 2001, there were over 7 million people living in Quebec—a quarter of Canada's population. About 80% of these residents, or *Québécois*, are native French speakers. Most trace their roots directly back to France. Only 8% say English is their native language. Even with new immigrants arriving, the province stays quite homogeneous compared with other Canadian provinces, and especially with a melting pot like the United States.

Unique Identity With its roots in 17th-century France and its branches in the global world of the 21st century, Quebec is a fascinating mix of times and places. Some people in the countryside still try to live the way their French ancestors did. Most of those in Montreal, though, would be at home in any city in the modern industrialized world.

Quebec's coat of arms captures this blending of contrasts. The shield includes France's fleur-de-lis, England's lion, and the federation of Canada's maple leaf. Inscribed below these symbols is the motto of the province—*Je me souviens* ("I remember"). The *Québécois* will never forget who they are and where they came from. As geographer Louis-Edmond Hamelin put it, "Quebec will continue to be North American, but it wants to speak French."

Now answer questions 1–6. Base your answers on the selection "Quebec: *Je me souviens.*"

1 Which sentence from the selection best summarizes its main idea?

A. It is also the oldest and largest of the Canadian provinces—and a unique crossroads of geography, cultures, languages, and people.

B. Quebec has given Canada four of its prime ministers, but the struggle for the province's political identity continues.

C. By the middle of the 19th century its population consisted of French (just under 80%), British (about 20%), and the rest a mix of native peoples and other ethnic groups.

D. Inscribed below these symbols is the motto of the province—*Je me souviens* ("I remember").

2 Read this statement from the selection:

With an area of 595,391 square miles, Quebec dwarfs France.

Which of the following statements best expresses its meaning?

A. France covers a much larger geographic area than Quebec does.

B. Quebec has the largest French population outside of France.

C. Quebec covers a much larger geographic area than France does.

D. Quebec is less important than France culturally.

3 What cause did the *Parti Québécois* stand for?

A. separate statehood for Quebec

B. banning the speaking of English in Quebec

C. preventing immigrants from entering Quebec

D. return of Quebec citizens to France

4 Which of the following best defines the word *homogeneous*?

 A. having more men than women

 B. politically stable

 C. intelligent

 D. made up of similar elements

5 Which of the following is NOT a benefit of the St. Lawrence Seaway?

 A. source of hydroelectric power

 B. climate regulator

 C. route for international shipping

 D. site for industry

6 How does Quebec's coat of arms express the province's unique identity?

THINKING IT THROUGH

The notes in the side columns will help you think through your answers. See the answer key at the bottom of the next page. How well did you do?

Remember that the main idea of the selection should be a broad statement about the topic. You can eliminate the three statements that focus on specific details about Quebec.

1 Which sentence from the selection best summarizes its main idea?

   A. It is also the oldest and largest of the Canadian provinces—and a unique crossroads of geography, cultures, languages, and people.

   B. Quebec has given Canada four of its prime ministers, but the struggle for the province's political identity continues.

   C. By the middle of the 19th century its population consisted of French (just under 80%), British (about 20%), and the rest a mix of native peoples and other ethnic groups.

   D. Inscribed below these symbols is the motto of the province—*Je me souviens* ("I remember").

Note that the highlighted sentence deals with land area, or size. So you can immediately eliminate answer choices B and D.

2 Read this statement from the selection:

   With an area of 595,391 square miles, Quebec dwarfs France.

   Which of the following statements best expresses its meaning?

   A. France covers a much larger geographic area than Quebec does.

   B. Quebec has the largest French population outside of France.

   C. Quebec covers a much larger geographic area than France does.

   D. Quebec is less important than France culturally.

Notice that three answer choices aren't mentioned in the discussion of the *Parti Québécois*. Skim the selection to find the issue the party fought for.

3 What cause did the *Parti Québécois* stand for?

   A. separate statehood for Quebec

   B. banning the speaking of English in Quebec

   C. preventing immigrants from entering Quebec

   D. return of Quebec citizens to France

4 Which of the following best defines the word *homogeneous*?

A. having more men than women

B. politically stable

C. intelligent

D. made up of similar elements

> Reread the paragraph containing the word *homogeneous*. Since that section deals with the heritage of the Quebec people, you can eliminate answer choices B and C. Then use context clues to find the correct answer.

5 Which of the following is NOT a benefit of the St. Lawrence Seaway?

A. source of hydroelectric power

B. climate regulator

C. route for international shipping

D. site for industry

> Pay attention to the key word in this question—*not*. Three of the answer choices are benefits of the St. Lawrence Seaway. Choose the one that has no relation to the river system.

6 How does Quebec's coat of arms express the province's unique identity?

> Quebec was first settled by the French, and then by the British and other people. Its coat of arms reflects this mixed heritage by including images of France, England, and Canada. Many of the French people in Quebec today have French roots, and they continue the fight to hold onto their culture and language. The motto on Quebec's coat of arms, "Je me souviens," is a reminder that Quebec will never forget its ties to France.

> This response received top marks because it:
> • addresses the question fully and stays on the topic.
> • is well-organized.
> • includes details and a quotation from the selection to support statements.
> • is written clearly, using correct grammar, punctuation, and spelling.

Answers:
1. A, 2. C, 3. A, 4. D, 5. B

**Note who the building
was built for.** How will
this information help you
understand the reputation of
the Paris Opera House?

**Pay attention to topic
sentences.** What new
information will this paragraph
tell you about the Paris Opera
House?

Reading Test Model
SHORT SELECTIONS

DIRECTIONS Use the following to practice your skills.
Read the paragraphs carefully. Then answer the
multiple-choice questions that follow.

The Paris Opera House

The Paris Opera House, also known as the
Opéra Garnier, Palais Garnier, and Théâtre
Nationale de l'Opéra, was designed by
Charles Garnier. He won a competition to
design it in 1860. It was built during the
Second Empire, between 1861 and 1875, for
Napoleon III.

It is a remarkable building in several
ways. In its heyday, it was a popular place
for the members of the French aristocracy to
gather. There was actually more space devoted
to socializing than to its massive 118,000-
square-foot stage. One favorite gathering place
was the Grand Staircase, a model of which can
be viewed at the Musée d'Orsay. The building
was renowned for its opulence. Its main
chandelier weighs six and half tons!

Today, the Opéra Garnier shows mostly
ballet. More operas are shown at the new
Opéra de la Bastille, a far larger and less well-
regarded building.

1 What was the author's purpose in writing the selection?

   A. To describe the history and significance of the Paris Opera House.

   B. To inform the reader about the career of French architect Charles Garnier.

   C. To entertain the reader with stories about the time of Napoleon III.

   D. To persuade the reader that the Opéra Garnier is better than the Opéra Bastille.

> **Understand the writer's purpose.** Persuading and entertaining are clearly incorrect choices. Which one covers the entire selection?

2 Which of the following is NOT a synonym for *opulent*?

   A. palatial

   B. precise

   C. lavish

   D. extravagant

> **Think about context.** The context of *opulent* is all about wealth and excess. Only three of the answer choices suggest these things.

Answers:
1. A, 2. B

READING STRATEGIES FOR ASSESSMENT

Read the title. What does the title tell you the chart is about?

_____

_____

Read the key. How does the key help you understand the numbers in the chart?

_____

_____

ANSWER STRATEGIES

> **Look for the lowest number.** The question refers to precipitation, or rainfall. The lowest number in that column will give you the correct answer.

> **Do the math.** Simple subtraction will give you the correct answer to question 4.

> **Read the numbers for July.** The correct answer has both the lowest minimum and the lowest maximum temperature in July.

DIRECTIONS Some test questions ask you to analyze a visual rather than a reading selection. Study this chart carefully and answer the questions that follow.

Climate of Selected French-Speaking Cities

City	January Temp. Max.	January Temp. Min.	July Temp. Max.	July Temp. Min.	Avg. Precip.
Casablanca, Morocco	62.8°	47.1°	77.7°	66.7°	16.8"
Geneva, Switzerland	38.3°	27.9°	76.3°	53.2°	35.6"
Montreal, Canada	21.6°	5.2°	79.2°	59.7°	37"
Paris, France	42.8°	33.6°	75.2°	55.2°	25.6"

Temperatures given in degrees Fahrenheit.
Source: _The World Almanac and Book of Facts,_ 2005

3 Which city has the driest climate?

A. Paris

B. Casablanca

C. Geneva

D. Montreal

4 Which city's maximum temperature varies the most between January and July?

A. Casablanca

B. Paris

C. Geneva

D. Montreal

5 Which city has the coldest temperature in July?

A. Geneva

B. Paris

C. Casablanca

D. Montreal

Answers:
3. B, 4. D, 5. A

Reading Test Practice
SHORT SELECTIONS

DIRECTIONS Use the following selection to practice your skills. Read the paragraphs carefully. Then answer the multiple-choice questions that follow.

The Musée d'Orsay

The Musée d'Orsay, a now famous museum in Paris, was once a train station. Before the 1900 World's Fair, government officials decided that a train station was needed in a more central location of the city. The location of the Palais d'Orsay was chosen as a site. Since the station would be near the Louvre and other important buildings, it had to be luxurious (especially for a train station). In 1898, Victor Laloux was chosen to build it. It was inaugurated during the Fair on July 14, 1900.

After 1939, the electrification of the train lines and other advances in train technology made the Gare d'Orsay obsolete. The building remained open for other uses until 1973, when it was closed.

The Musée d'Orsay opened in 1987. The design team was directed to respect Laloux's original style while transforming the space into a world-class venue for showing great 20th-century art. Works are shown on three main levels. Separate rooms are accessible on each level. This makes the museum a quite different experience from the huge, hallway-centric Louvre. The museum receives over two million visitors a year.

1 Which of the following does NOT describe the Musée d'Orsay?

A. It is inside an old train station.

B. It showcases art of the 20th century.

C. It opened in the year 1987.

D. It is very similar to the Louvre.

2 Which of the following helps explain the closing of the Gare d'Orsay?

A. The train station was never intended to last beyond the World's Fair.

B. The train station cost too much to maintain.

C. New technologies made the train station obsolete.

D. New technologies made it cheaper to build other train stations.

DIRECTIONS Some test questions ask you to analyze a visual rather than a reading selection. Study this chart carefully and answer the questions that follow

Medal Standings, Francophone Games 2001

	Gold	Silver	Bronze
Canada	12	8	18
France	13	11	8
Madagascar	1	4	3
Senegal	1	1	1

Medal Standings, Francophone Games 1997

	Gold	Silver	Bronze
Canada	10	14	13
France	23	23	15
Madagascar	15	6	15
Senegal	5	1	6

Source: *http://jeux.francophonie.org*

3 How many total medals did Canada win in 2001?

A. 12

B. 37

C. 38

D. 42

4 In 1997 and 2001 combined, how many gold and silver medals did Madagascar win?

A. 21

B. 26

C. 36

D. 44

5 How many more bronze medals did Senegal win in 1997 than in 2001?

A. 5

B. 8

C. 3

D. 4

THINKING IT THROUGH

The notes in the side columns will help you think through your answers. Check the key at the bottom of the page. How well did you do?

Notice the word in capital letters in the question. Then ask yourself which of the answer choices is not supported by information in the selection.

1 Which of the following does NOT describe the Musée d'Orsay?

   A. It is inside an old train station.

   B. It showcases art of the 20th century.

   C. It opened in the year 1987.

   D. It is very similar to the Louvre.

If you reread the selection carefully, you'll easily be able to eliminate all but the correct answer choice.

2 Which of the following helps explain the closing of the Gare d'Orsay?

   A. The train station was never intended to last beyond the World's Fair.

   B. The train station cost too much to maintain.

   C. New technologies made the train station obsolete.

   D. New technologies made it cheaper to build other train stations.

Read across carefully to find the numbers you need. Add them together to get the correct answer.

3 How many total medals did Canada win in 2001?

   A. 12

   B. 37

   C. 38

   D. 42

Determine the totals for each year. Then add your totals together.

4 In 1997 and 2001 combined, how many gold and silver medals did Madagascar win?

   A. 21

   B. 26

   C. 36

   D. 44

5 How many more bronze medals did Senegal win in 1997 than in 2001?

A. 5

B. 8

C. 3

D. 4

To answer this question, subtract the 2001 number from the 1997 number. Make sure your information comes from the correct column and row.

Functional Reading Test Model

DIRECTIONS Study the following guide to storing contacts on a mobile phone. Then answer the questions that follow.

Storing Contacts on Your Mobile Phone

You can use the Contacts directory on your mobile phone to maintain information about an individual or a company. You should be able to store around 150 contacts. Just follow these five easy steps.

Entering and Storing a New Contact

1. Enter the phone number you want to store.
2. Press ⓞⓀ to select **New Save.**
3. Enter the contact's name. For information on entering text in English or Spanish, see page 35.
4. Press ⓞⓀ to select **Save.** Or press ⟨⟩ **Right** and then press ⓞⓀ to select **Options.** Press ⟨⟩ **Up** or **Down** to select one of the following options:
   - **Save** This will save your information.
   - **Type of Number** This will identify the number as **work, home, fax, pager,** or **mobile.**
   - **Use Voice Recognition** Clearly say the name of the contact. This will enable you to dial the number using our exclusive voice recognition software.
   - **Speed Dial** You can select a speed dial code number from the list of available code numbers.
   - **Password Protected** If you select **yes,** the contact will be blocked from view. To view or edit the contact, you first have to enter your three-digit password.
5. Finally, press ⓞⓀ to select **Save.** The message *Contact Saved!* will appear on the viewing screen.

READING STRATEGIES FOR ASSESSMENT

Read the guide carefully. The steps are listed in chronological order. Notice that Step 4 offers two choices. If you select the second choice, you are presented with a list of options. Circle these options.

Interpret symbols. Circle each symbol in the guide. Be sure you understand what each symbol means.

1. How can you access the option that lets you use voice recognition?

   A. Press ⊙K.

   B. See page 35.

   C. Press ⟨⟩ **Right**, then press ⊙K to select **Options**.

   D. Enter your three-digit password.

2. When must you use your three-digit password?

   A. to view or edit a blocked contact

   B. to speed dial a number

   C. to save a new contact

   D. to use voice recognition

3. How can you speed dial a contact?

   A. Enter the number and then press ⊙K.

   B. Enter your three-digit password.

   C. Press ⊙K and select **Speed Dial**.

   D. Assign a special code number to the contact.

Answers:
1. C, 2. A, 3. D

DIRECTIONS Study the following prescription label. Circle the information that you think is the most important. Then answer the multiple–choice questions that follow.

Lalonde Pharmacy
1700 West 19th Street
Chicago IL 60618
PH (773) 555-0168

Patient PH   (773) 555-7462

Alicia Dufresne
3535 N. Summerdale
Chicago IL 60641

NO: 01448-78124
DATE: 8/26/07

Cozon 50 mg tablets

TAKE ONE TABLET DAILY AT BREAKFAST

QTY: 30
REFILLS: 4

DR. M. de Valle

TAKE WITH FOOD

WARNING: Do not drive or operate heavy
machinery while taking this medication.

1 How long will this prescription last with refills?

A. 1 month

B. 5 months

C. 2 months

D. 6 months

2 How many milligrams of medicine must Madame Dufresne take each day?

A. 30 mg

B. 4 mg

C. 50 mg

D. 40 mg

3 What must Madame Dufresne do if she doesn't eat breakfast one day?

A. skip the dose that day

B. take the dose later in the day

C. take the dose with food, perhaps a snack

D. take two doses the next day

THINKING IT THROUGH

The notes in the side column will help you think through your answers. Check the answer key at the bottom of the page. How well did you do?

> Multiply the number of pills by the number of refills and add the original number of pills to determine how long the prescription will last.

1 How long will this prescription last with refills?

A. 1 month

B. 5 months

C. 2 months

D. 6 months

> Read the label carefully. Each pill is 50 mg, and the directions say to take one each day.

2 How many milligrams of medicine must Madame Dufresne take each day?

A. 30 mg

B. 4 mg

C. 50 mg

D. 40 mg

> Each dose should be taken in the morning with food. It won't matter whether the dose is taken with breakfast or with a snack as long as it is taken in the morning.

3 What must Madame Dufresne do if she doesn't eat breakfast one day?

A. skip the dose that day

B. take the dose later in the day

C. take the dose with food, perhaps a snack

D. take two doses the next day

Revising-and-Editing Test Model

DIRECTIONS Read the following paragraph carefully. Then answer the multiple-choice questions that follow. After answering the questions, read the material in the side columns to check your answer strategies.

¹ Last summer my cousins and me visited Canada and we spent a morning in Old Quebec. ² We seen a brochure that said it would be 400 years old in 2008! ³ It was the center of New France during the 17th and 18th centuries. ⁴ It was known as the center of French culture. ⁵ In the Western Hemisphere. ⁶ Because of its history and architecture, UNESCO declared Old Quebec a World Heritage Site. ⁷ We would of stayed longer, but our bus was leaving for the return trip to Montreal. ⁸ We plan to go to Old Quebec again one day. ⁹ We plan to explore the city further.

ANSWER STRATEGIES

1 Which of the following is the best way to rewrite the beginning of sentence 1?

    A. Last summer, us cousins…

    B. Last summer, my cousins and I…

    C. Last summer, me and my cousins…

    D. Last summer, I and my cousins…

Personal Pronouns When deciding whether to use the personal pronoun *me* or *I* in a sentence, think about how the pronoun is used. If it's used as the subject, use *I*. If it's used as an object, use *me*.

2 What is the correct way to punctuate the two complete thoughts in sentence 1?

    A. …visited Canada: and we…

    B. …visited Canada; and we…

    C. …visited Canada, and we…

    D. …visited Canada–and we…

Correct Punctuation Sentence 1 is a compound sentence. That is, it has two independent clauses joined by the conjunction *and*. In such cases, the correct punctuation is a comma.

3 Which of the following errors do you find in sentence 2?

A. incorrect verb tense

B. incorrect capitalization

C. unclear pronoun reference

D. misspelled word

4 Which sentence in the paragraph is a fragment?

A. sentence 4

B. sentence 2

C. sentence 9

D. sentence 5

5 Which of the following is the best way to rewrite the beginning of sentence 7?

A. We would have stayed longer…

B. We could of stayed longer…

C. We woulda stayed longer…

D. We coulda stayed longer…

6 What is the best way to combine sentences 8 and 9?

A. We plan to go to Old Quebec again one day, and we plan to explore the city further.

B. We plan to go to Old Quebec again one day and explore the city further.

C. We plan to go to Old Quebec again one day; and we plan to explore the city further.

D. We plan to go to Old Quebec again one day, and explore the city further.

Answers:
1. B, 2. C, 3. A, 4. D, 5. A, 6. B

Revising-and-Editing Test Practice

DIRECTIONS Read the following paragraph carefully. As you read, circle each error that you find and identify the error in the side column—for example, *misspelled word* or *incorrect punctuation*. When you have finished, circle the letter of the correct choice for each question that follows.

¹ On April 4 1914 in Gia Dinh Vietnam, Marguerite Duras was born. ² By the end of the 20th century, Duras was recognized as one of the most finest women writers in all of France. ³ Her first successful novel was published in 1950 it was called *Un barrage contre le Pacifique* (*The Sea Wall*). ⁴ She wrote the screenplay for the film *Hiroshima mon amour*. ⁵ Duras' novel *L'Amant* won a French literary prize in 1984. ⁶ The *Prix Goncourt,* one of the most significant prizes authors can win in France.

1 What is the correct way to punctuate the first part of sentence 1?

A. On April, 4, 1914 in Gia Dinh, Vietnam,

B. On April 4, 1914, in Gia Dinh, Vietnam,

C. On April 4, 1914, in Gia Dinh Vietnam,

D. On April 4 1914, in Gia Dinh, Vietnam,

2 Which of the following is the correct superlative to use in sentence 2?

A. finer

B. more finer

C. most finer

D. finest

3 Sentence 3 is a run-on. Which of the following is the best way to fix it?

   A. Her first successful novel was published in 1950 and it was called *Un barrage contre le Pacifique (The Sea Wall)*.

   B. Her first successful novel was published in 1950. It was called *Un barrage contre le Pacifique (The Sea Wall)*.

   C. Her first successful novel was published in 1950: it was called *Un barrage contre le Pacifique (The Sea Wall)*.

   D. Her first successful novel was published in 1950; and it was called *Un barrage contre le Pacifique (The Sea Wall)*.

4 Which resource would you consult to find a more interesting word for called in sentence 3?

   A. dictionary

   B. glossary

   C. encyclopedia

   D. thesaurus

5 Which of the following is the correct singular possessive form of *Duras* in sentence 5?

   A. Duras's

   B. Duras'

   C. Duras's'

   D. Duras'es

6 Which sentence in the paragraph is actually a fragment?

   A. sentence 1

   B. sentence 4

   C. sentence 5

   D. sentence 6

THINKING IT THROUGH

Use the notes in the side columns to help you understand why some answers are correct and others are not. Check the answer key on the next page. How well did you do?

1 What is the correct way to punctuate the first part of sentence 1?

    A. On April, 4, 1914 in Gia Dinh, Vietnam,

    B. On April 4, 1914, in Gia Dinh, Vietnam,

    C. On April 4, 1914, in Gia Dinh Vietnam,

    D. On April 4 1914, in Gia Dinh, Vietnam,

> When writing dates, the day and the year are separated by commas and the year is separated from the rest of the sentence by a comma. When writing a place name, the city is separated from a country by a comma, and the country is separated from the rest of the sentence by a comma.

2 Which of the following is the correct superlative to use in sentence 2?

    A. finer

    B. more finer

    C. most finer

    D. finest

> The superlative form of an adjective or adverb can be formed in two ways. Either the word ends in -*est*, or the word is preceded by *most*. *Most* and the -*est* ending are never used together.

3 Sentence 3 is a run-on. Which of the following is the best way to fix it?

    A. Her first successful novel was published in 1950 and it was called *Un barrage contre le Pacifique (The Sea Wall).*

    B. Her first successful novel was published in 1950. It was called *Un barrage contre le Pacifique (The Sea Wall).*

    C. Her first successful novel was published in 1950: it was called *Un barrage contre le Pacifique (The Sea Wall).*

    D. Her first successful novel was published in 1950; and it was called *Un barrage contre le Pacifique (The Sea Wall).*

> The best way to fix this run-on sentence is just to divide it into two simple sentences.

A thesaurus is a book of synonyms (words with similar meanings).

4 Which resource would you consult to find a more interesting word for *called* in sentence 3?

A. dictionary

B. glossary

C. encyclopedia

D. thesaurus

The singular possessive is formed by adding an apostrophe and *-s* to the word.

5 Which of the following is the correct singular possessive form of *Duras* in sentence 5?

A. Duras's

B. Duras'

C. Duras's'

D. Duras'es

Remember that a sentence fragment is missing either a subject or a verb and does not express a complete thought.

6 Which sentence in the paragraph is actually a fragment?

A. sentence 1

B. sentence 4

C. sentence 5

D. sentence 6

Writing Test Model

DIRECTIONS Many tests ask you to write an essay in response to a writing prompt. A writing prompt is a brief statement that describes a writing situation. Some writing prompts ask you to explain *what, why,* or *how.* Others ask you to convince someone of something.

As you analyze the following writing prompts, read and respond to the notes in the side columns. Then look at the response to each prompt. The notes in the side columns will help you understand why each response is considered strong.

ANALYZING THE PROMPT

Identify the topic. Read the first paragraph of the prompt carefully. Underline the topic of the essay you will write.

Understand what's expected of you. The second paragraph of the prompt explains what you must do and offers suggestions on how to create a successful response.

Prompt A

Everyone enjoys leisure time and everyone has a favorite way to enjoy such time. Think about what you like to do most with your leisure time.

Now write an essay that describes your favorite leisure activity. Include details that enable readers to understand and experience your enthusiasm.

Strong Response

Between school and working at my family's hardware store, I don't have much time to myself. However, when I can grab a couple of hours of free time, I love jumping on my bike and riding the back roads just outside of Carpentersville. Whether I'm alone or with friends, a long ride helps clear my mind and refresh my spirit.

I ride a road bike, a lightweight, sleek machine with a red pearl finish. Its drop handlebars, thin tires, and sixteen gears are perfect for propelling me along the gently rolling hills of these parts. I've devised several different routes through the countryside. Some are designed for speed—perfect for those days when I'm looking for a really good workout. Other routes are more scenic. I can take these

ANSWER STRATEGIES

Grab the reader's attention. This opening paragraph is an invitation to the reader to go riding with the writer and experience what he experiences on his bike.

Provide interesting information. Here the writer describes his bike and the routes he takes, painting a picture for the reader.

at a slower pace and often choose them when I've got some thinking to do or when I just want to enjoy a beautiful day.

I also like the rituals of bike riding. I'm always tinkering with my bike, lubricating the gearing, adjusting the brakes, and making sure everything is screwed together tightly. Then there's the clothing: padded bike shorts, brightly colored jersey, leather-and-gel riding gloves, special shoes that attach securely to the pedals, and an aerodynamic helmet that matches the bike's finish. Sometimes I feel like an astronaut suiting up for a shuttle launch. Finally there are the accessories. I always carry a repair kit in case of breakdowns, a mini-pump for flat tires, and a medical kit in case of spills. My favorite accessory, though, is my trip computer. It tells me how fast I'm traveling and how far I've gone. It even monitors my heart rate!

Some of my friends think I'm a little obsessed with bike riding. Maybe they're right. But when I'm zooming down a long hill or leaning into a soft curve, feeling the wind rushing past, I experience a kind of joy and contentment that I can't get from anything else.

Use effective topic sentences. The writer lets the reader know that this paragraph will be about the rituals of biking, prompting the reader to wonder just what those rituals are.

Include specific details. Words like *padded, brightly colored, leather-and-gel, special,* and *aerodynamic* bring the writer's details to life.

Reinforce the major point. In the conclusion, the writer repeats his enthusiasm for bike riding.

Prompt B

Since the mid-1990s, federal law has required television manufacturers to install a so-called "v-chip" in every television they produce. The v-chip allows the user to block certain channels unless a password is entered. The purpose of the v-chip legislation was to give parents control over what their children could access on television, whether the parents were present or not.

Think about the purpose of the v-chip. Do you agree or disagree with the law that made it mandatory? Is it useful technology for parents, or does it unfairly limit what children can watch? Write an essay in which you state your opinion and provide convincing arguments to support that opinion.

Strong Response

My family recently installed a satellite dish on the roof of our house. We now have access to over 200 television channels. Most of the programming on these channels is harmless: cartoons, sitcoms, sports, cooking, home improvement, and so on. Some of the channels, however, present programming that is suitable only for adults. I believe the government was right to insist that television manufacturers install v-chip technology so that parents can block unwanted programming if they choose to.

I am sixteen years old, and my younger sisters are eight and twelve years old. Our parents try to pay close attention to what we watch on television, but that's not always possible. For example, when my parents go out for the evening and I'm at home taking care

ANALYZING THE PROMPT

Identify the topic. The first paragraph of the prompt makes it clear that the topic is v-chip technology.

Know what's expected of you. The second paragraph of the prompt lets you know that you're going to write an essay in which you take a position and provide arguments to support that position.

ANSWER STRATEGIES

Engage the reader's interest. The writer begins on a personal note to draw the reader into the essay.

State the position clearly. The last sentence of the introductory paragraph states the writer's position clearly and forcefully.

Begin supporting the position. The writer begins supporting her position by acknowledging that even well-intentioned parents can't be everywhere.

of my sisters, there are no adults to supervise what we watch on tv.

Sometimes, unsuitable programming can show up on the screen even when you're not looking for it. You might be channel surfing with no particular program in mind and suddenly stumble across a program clearly intended for adults. Until the government acted, there was nothing parents could do about such accidental discoveries.

With v-chip technology, however, parents can take action. Using simple, on-screen prompts, parents can block access to any channels they don't want their children to see. These channels might present adult programming, excessively violent programming, movies that my be suitable for some children but not for others, and so on.

My parents told me when our dish was being installed that they intended to block a number of channels they felt were not suitable for our family. At first I thought that was unfair, but the more I thought about it, the more I realized my parents were just doing their job as parents. I don't know how many channels they blocked, and I don't really care. We've still got about 175 channels to watch, and that's plenty for any family.

Use language that echoes the prompt. The phrase "until the government acted" reminds readers of the topic introduced in the prompt.

Expand the argument. The writer adds to her argument by noting that adult programming is just one type of programming that parents might find offensive or unsuitable.

Acknowledge other points of view. The writer admits that at first she was against the idea of blocking channels but now understands why parents find this technology useful.

Writing Test Practice

DIRECTIONS Read the following writing prompt. Using the strategies you've learned in this section, analyze the prompt, plan your response, and then write an essay explaining your position.

Prompt C

Due to a serious budget crisis, your school district must find ways to save money. The school board has decided to lay off some teachers and increase the number of students in each class by five to ten students.

Think about the effect additional students in each class will have on students and teachers. Has the school board made a sound decision in your opinion? Write a letter to the board that explains why you favor or oppose their decision. State your position clearly and provide persuasive supporting arguments.

Scoring Rubrics

DIRECTIONS Use the following checklist to see whether you have written a strong persuasive essay. You will have succeeded if you can check nearly all of the items.

The Prompt

☐ My response meets all the requirements stated in the prompt.

☐ I have stated my position clearly and supported it with details.

☐ I have addressed the audience appropriately.

☐ My essay fits the type of writing suggested in the prompt (letter to the editor, article for the school paper, and so on).

Reasons

☐ The reasons I offer really support my position.

☐ My audience will find the reasons convincing.

☐ I have stated my reasons clearly.

☐ I have given at least three reasons.

☐ I have supported my reasons with sufficient facts, examples, quotations, and other details.

☐ I have presented and responded to opposing arguments.

☐ My reasoning is sound. I have avoided faulty logic.

Order and Arrangement

☐ I have included a strong introduction.

☐ I have included a strong conclusion.

☐ The reasons are arranged in a logical order.

Word Choice

☐ The language of my essay is appropriate for my audience.

☐ I have used precise, vivid words and persuasive language.

Fluency

☐ I have used sentences of varying lengths and structures.

☐ I have connected ideas with transitions and other devices.

☐ I have used correct spelling, punctuation, and grammar.

Notes

Notes

Notes

Notes

Notes

Notes

Notes

Notes

Notes

Notes

Notes

Notes

Notes

Notes

Credits

Acknowledgments

"Chanson de la Seine" from *Spectacle* by Jacques Prévert. Text copyright © 1951 by Éditions Gallimard. Reprinted by permission of Editions Gallimard and Société FATRAS.

"Couplet de la rue de Bagnolet" from *Destinée Arbitraire* by Robert Desnos. Text copyright © Éditions Gallimard. Reprinted by permission of Éditions Gallimard.

Photography

159 (cl) Ivy Close Images/Alamy; **169** (tr) ©Douglas Peebles Photography/Alamy; **171** (tc) Comstock/Getty Images; **173** (t) Comstock/Getty Images.